team
basketball
offense and defense

The Star & The Columbia Record,
staff photo by Richard Taylor

team
basketball
offense and defense

Comprising *Offensive Basketball*
and *Defensive Basketball*

Frank McGuire

**Head Coach of Basketball
University of South Carolina**

prentice-hall, inc.
Englewood Cliffs, New Jersey

Offensive Basketball © 1958, *Defensive Basketball* © 1959, *Team Basketball: Offense and Defense* © 1966 by Prentice-Hall, Inc., Englewood Cliffs, New Jersey. All rights reserved. No part of this book may be reproduced in any form or by any means without permission in writing from the publisher.

Library of Congress Catalog Card No.: 66-28119
Printed in the United States of America   C-89677

Current Printing (last digit):

10   9   8   7   6   5   4   3   2   1

Prentice-Hall International, Inc., *London*
Prentice-Hall of Australia, Pty. Ltd., *Sydney*
Prentice-Hall of Canada, Ltd., *Toronto*
Prentice-Hall of India (Private) Ltd., *New Delhi*
Prentice-Hall of Japan, Inc., *Tokyo*

to
my wife
Pat
always an inspiration

and to
Clair Bee
a close and treasured friend

Ben Carnevale (left) and Frank McGuire

foreword

Writing this foreword is a most pleasant task for me. First, because my very good friend and colleague, Frank McGuire, asked me to do it; second, because it concerns the great game of basketball.

My association and friendship with Frank goes back more than thirty years. And, appropriately, it all started with the game of basketball. Our relationship started as college and professional opponents, and then continued as teammates in professional play, as high school coaches, as assistant coaches to each other, and as college coaches but, fundamentally, as true friends. Consequently, when I say that Frank is more than a student, teacher, coach, and lecturer of basketball, I feel qualified to speak.

It is my personal opinion that this book will be a great contribution to basketball, not only to coaches, but to players, spectators, officials, and all those interested in the game. Frank's entire philosophy of basketball and life is wrapped up in this book. It has been my privilege to have talked with, and listened to, Frank concerning his ideas and theories of offensive and defensive basketball.

Frank's basketball beginnings and education were dominated by the New York City environment in which he was born and bred. His knowledge of the game was gained the hard way. He first played and fought on the playgrounds where the playing areas were congested, where a basketball was a prize to be fought for and where the competition was intense and cruel.

The so-called "Eastern Style" offense dominated. This type of offense consisted then, as now, of the give-and-go cutting style; the one-on-one, man-to-man matchups; fast, accurate passing; quick, expert foot-work and the "picks" and screens so closely associated with basketball when played in close quarters.

A terrific amount of personal pride was involved in "getting free" from the leeching defense of the player assigned to guard (shut out) the offensive player and in keeping down the scoring of the opponent against whom the defensive player was matched. This "matchup" and man-to-man type of play, naturally, left its mark on Frank and it has always been reflected in his coaching.

As far back as I can remember, Frank McGuire has been a defense-minded coach. He may not always have had the necessary material, but you can be sure that a great deal of defensive thought and theory went into each and every one of his big games. I was fortunate enough to ac-company his St. John's team to Seattle in 1952. At that time he was faced with the problem of defensing Clyde Lovellette, Kansas' six-foot-ten-inch star, one of the great centers of that era. Then, in 1957, as coach of the North Carolina Tar Heels, it was seven-foot-two-inch Wilt Chamberlain and another fine Kansas team. In both instances, Frank's defensive plans and strategies were efficient and successful.

Frank is a consistent exponent of the use of varied defenses. He is not afraid to make changes or alter his plans when the situation arises. Frank can defense an opponent more soundly than any other coach I have known.

I know that all who read this book will greatly increase their knowl-edge of basketball and will become intimately acquainted with Frank McGuire—not only as a coach, teacher, and writer, but as a leader of youth, a man who is devoted to his family, his friends, and his profession.

BEN CARNEVALE
Director of Athletics
New York University

preface

An old maxim exists which states that a coach is no better than his players. The truth of this axiom has been proven time and again. Being an eternal optimist—what coach isn't—I like to dream that some season when I don't have the material, I can somehow mould the boys into such a unit and fire them up with such a spirit that we can win in spite of the lack of material. In fact, in a few rare instances, coaches have been able to pull off such miracles. But I have been at the game long enough to know that such dreams don't often materialize. The best a coach can hope for year after year is not to pull off a miracle, but to realize the potential of the material with which he has to work. A coach never looks bad when he has an ordinary season with weak material, but he certainly does with strong material.

All I am trying to say is that I have been coaching long enough to realize the vital importance of the players. I hope I never become so self-centered that I forget that fact. Most of my time is devoted to finding a few boys who will fit, temperamentally and physically, into my system. There are, I am quick to add, hundreds and even thousands of high school graduates each year who can play excellent college ball. But, early in their careers all coaches and players fall into certain definite patterns. As a result, many fine players, through no fault of their own, just will not fit into a different system. The successful coach, therefore, must be able to recognize—and he frequently doesn't have much time—the boys who can play his style of basketball.

At this point, of course, there is a great deal of luck involved. We can—and frequently do—make mistakes. The player fails to develop, or he won't work, or he thinks too slowly, or he gets hurt, or he becomes homesick and goes home, or he can't pass his school work. These and other related problems insure coaches gray hairs and stomach ulcers long before their time. All any coach can do is try to eliminate as many of these difficulties as possible.

By now, I know pretty well the type of boys I want for my system and I try as hard as I can to get them interested in playing under my direction. This is only a part of it. It is necessary to interest them in the University of South Carolina and to be reasonably certain that they can not only pass South Carolina's entrance examinations, but that they can maintain the scholastic average that the University requires for good standing. That, as all coaches know, is a grave problem. Even when we secure thoroughly capable students, we sometimes have a hard time making them understand that academic competence comes first in importance.

Many prep school stars, potentially fine students, fall by the way because their chief interest is in sports alone. For the most part, however, this problem solves itself once the boys get settled. They invariably like the school and the town so well that they are more than willing to do whatever work is necessary to make a place for themselves in the school as students. I came to South Carolina University from New York City and since I planned, in the beginning, at least, to look there for my material, I thought the problem of acclimating the boys might prove serious. Actually, this has never been a problem.

As every college coach knows, basketball in many parts of the country is characterized by certain pecularities of style developed through tradition, coaching, weather conditions, playgrounds, and so on. And a coach like me often feels that he is better off to find boys who have played under conditions and in a style which he is best acquainted. As a result, I have tried to find my material in and around New York. Not only do I know the system played there, but I understand the thinking of the boys since that is my home area. I am not foolish enough to think, of course, that boys from the City can run any faster or jump any higher than others, but I understand them better, and what is even more important, they understand me.

Since I have coached and played high school basketball, I am familiar with the problems of the high school mentor. I am keenly aware that he cannot seek out boys who are familiar with and schooled in his style of play. He must work with the boys who come to him up through the lower grades and his problem is concerned primarily with the *development* of players to fit into his style of play.

The high school coach must, therefore, devise a system, a feeder system, up through the grades, the playgrounds, the Y.M.C.A. and the Y.M.H.A, and the community organizations and centers, which will provide the type of player he desires. This system calls for a complete organization of all "home-town" coaches to provide a certain type of player. It is at this point that the personality and salesmanship of the coach becomes invaluable. He must become the home-town ambassador of basketball and rally the grade school and other home-town coaches behind his program. It means hard work and long hours but will result in good players trained in the fundamentals and versed in the style of basketball the coach desires.

All coaches appreciate the importance of defensive basketball. Unfortunately, the players tend to show more interest in the offense. Spectators, too, have become geared to high scoring games. Individual and team defense has been forced into the background.

Defense can be the equalizer in basketball for the player who may not have the fine skills necessary for high scoring. By intense desire, hard work, and aggressiveness, most boys can learn to play good defense regardless of any lack in shooting ability. And, once he has mastered good defensive play, a boy will generally find a place on a team (especially at the University of South Carolina, where special emphasis is placed on good defensive play).

As a player, the writer's first love was defense; it was the principal reason he was selected to play professional basketball. Ideally, I would like to have five players who could play good individual man-to-man defense, each blessed with tremendous pride in his ability to defense his man. Then it would never be necessary to debate before each game— "Which defense or defensive combination shall I use against this team?"

A coach can relax if he has five good defensive men. His team will be consistent in its use of the most important part of the game; he need not give up if his team has an "off-shooting" night.

Today, however, players are so engrossed in offensive play that all coaches—high school, college and professional—must utilize a number of variations to compensate for defensive weaknesses.

While individual defense has not declined since the low-scoring days of basketball, it has not improved as rapidly as individual offense (with its jump and hook shots). In order to combat the effectiveness of these individual offensive maneuvers, a tremendous amount of emphasis has been placed on *team* defense. Team defense has been the basis of a defensive improvement almost as great as the success with new offenses. In the last few years more unique team defensive combinations have been shown across the country than in the many preceding years of basketball.

The number of set defenses today greatly outnumbers the number of offenses. Most team defenses are based on two premises:

1. Since the defense cannot expect to hold the opponents scoreless, they must "play the percentages" and prevent the offensive team from doing what they do best. This has led to the development of the many defensive variations covered in this text. Coaches now plan ahead, preparing their players individually and as a team, to utilize a special defense to check the opponent who has superior players or a strong, effective attack.

2. A coach must use the element of surprise so that the opponents will not know what defensive moves to expect. This applies at the beginning of and throughout the game. Thus, team defenses may change on each play, as in modern football.

In addition to Clair Bee, the author wishes to acknowledge his indebtedness to the following people:

Coach James "Buck" Freeman, my college coach at St. John's University and presently my assistant at South Carolina University.

Herman Maison, Editor, Scholastic Coach Magazine, Vic Tuttle and Richard Taylor, of *The Columbia Record*, William Prouty, of *The Chapel Hill Weekly*, for their kind permission to use their photographs in this book.

The players at the Universities of North and South Carolina, who posed for many of the pictures.

Mrs. Jean Keller, secretary at the University of North Carolina Athletic Association.

Dean Smith, former player at Kansas University, who is presently head coach at North Carolina University.

FRANK McGUIRE

contents

1
coaching principles
and philosophies
1

A COACHING CODE, 1; General perspective, 1; Faculty standing, 1; Training and health, 1; School loyalty, 2; Public relations, 2; Publicity, 2; Sportsmanship, 2; Rules, 3; Professional interest, 2; Player-coach relationship, 4; The team, 4; Fundamentals, 4; Leadership, 5; Practice programs, 5; The coach, 6; MY BASKETBALL PHILOSOPHY, 7; The player, 7; The team, 8; Coaching, 9; Practices, 10; The offense, 10; The defense, 11; The game, 12; PLANNING THE SEASON, 12; Pre-season, 12; Gymnasium and equipment, 13; The captain, 13; Managers, 13; Staff meetings, 14; Squad meetings, 14; Conditioning, 14; Early season (first two weeks of practice), 15; In season, 16; Training rules, 16

2
building a style
of play
19

THE SOUTH CAROLINA OFFENSE, 19; The Two-Three, 19; ADVANCING THE BALL, 20; THE FAST BREAK, 22; GIVE-AND-GO WEAVE, 30; UTILIZING THE BIG MAN, 33; THE BIG MAN IN PROFESSIONAL BASKETBALL, 35; BIG MAN OFFENSE, 37; POSITIONS, 38; Pivot man in position 1, 39; Pivot man in position 2, 39; Pivot man in position 3, 40; Big man in position 4, 40; *THE DOUBLE PIVOT,* 40; Double-pivot in position 1, 40; Pivot in position 1 and post in position 4, 41; *THE FIVE-MAN GIVE-AND-GO WEAVE,* 41; *THE FIVE-MAN ROLL,* 43; *THE FOUR-MAN ROLL WITH A POST-PIVOT,* 44

3
basic offenses versus
man-to-man defense
49

THE TWO-THREE OFFENSE, 49; *THE ONE-TWO-TWO OFFENSE,* 62

4
the basic
zone offenses
79

THE ONE-THREE-ONE ZONE OFFENSE, 81; Position requirements, 81; Attacking the Two-Three zone defenses, 81; Attacking the Two-One-Two zone defense, 83; Attacking the One-Three-One zone defense, 84; Two-Two-One Offense, 86; Attacking the One-Two-Two zone defense, 87; Attacking the Three-Two zone defense, 89; Attacking the Two-One-Two zone defense, 89

5
offensive game
situations
91

GAME SIGNALS, 91; *JUMP-BALL TEAM PLAY,* 93; *OUT-OF-BOUNDS PLAYS,* 95; *PLAYING THE LANE,* 100; *THE CONTROL GAME,* 100; *FREEZING THE BALL,* 102; *MEETING THE PRESS,* 104; *ATTACKING THE SAG AND THE FLOAT,* 107; *ATTACKING DEFENSIVE VARIATIONS,* 108

6
defensive philosophies
and principles
111

A DEFENSIVE PHILOSOPHY, 111; The importance of defense, 112; Good defense is consistent, 113; High school teams and defense, 114; *A DEFENSIVE CODE,* 115; Man-to-man is basic defense, 115; Each player must do his job, 117

7
man-to-man
team defense
119

DEFENSIVE TEAM PRINCIPLES, 119; Four basic principles, 119; Defensive areas, 120; Defensive court balance, 122; Retreating methods, 124; DEFENSIVE TEAM VARIATIONS, 124; Sagging and floating, 125; Closing the gate, 125; TEAM PROBLEM OF THE BIG MAN, 126; Playing between the ball and the man, 128; Playing the pivot man three-quarters, 128; Double-teaming, 128; Using a collapsing defense, 129; Using a zone defense, 129; The full-court press, 129; SPECIAL MAN-TO-MAN TEAM DEFENSES, 130; Offensive defense, 130; Loose man-to-man defense, 131; COLLAPSING MAN-TO-MAN DEFENSE, 131; Rebounding, 132; STOPPING THE FAST BREAK, 133; The tactics of the offense, 133; The tactics of the defense, 134; South Carolina's tactics, 134; SUPPORT MAN-TO-MAN DEFENSE, 139

8
the zone defenses
147

INTRODUCTION, 147; The box-and-one zone defense, 147; THE SOUTH CAROLINA UNIVERSITY POINT ZONE DEFENSE, 149; Responsibilities of each position, 151; POINT-AND-ONE DEFENSE, 155

9
combination defenses
159

THE SCREEN-SWITCH DEFENSE, 159; One-man zone defense, 161; Box and One, 162

10
defensive game
situations
165

PLAYING THE LANE, 165; JUMP-BALL AND OUT-OF-BOUNDS PLAYS, 168; Jump-ball defense, 168; Checking out-of-bounds plays, 173; MEETING THE FREEZE AND THE STALL, 176; The freeze, 176; The stall, 177

11
the press
and its variations
179

INTRODUCTION, 179; THE FULL-COURT PRESS, 180; Apply the press, 180; VARIATIONS OF THE PRESS, 183; Single-man press, 183; The two-man press, 183; Three-quarter press, 184; Semi-press, 186; The zone press, 186; The South Carolina combination press, 188

12
game organization,
strategy, and scouting
191

Organization for game day, 191; Locker room details, 193; Pre-game practice, 193; OFFENSIVE GAME PROCEDURE, 193; Style of game to be played, 194; The first time-out, 194; Substitutions, 195; Between halves, 195; Decisions, 196; DEFENSIVE GAME PROCEDURE, 197; Matching players, 198; Getting the ball, 198; Coach's defense check list, 199; Scouting, 200; Scouting individual opponents, 204; Personal scouting, 204; Staff scouting, 204; Scouting services, 205; Conclusion, 205

index
207

team
basketball
offense and defense

key to charts

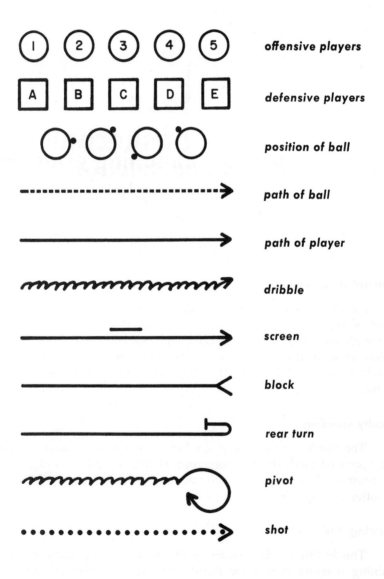

① ② ③ ④ ⑤	offensive players
A B C D E	defensive players
	position of ball
	path of ball
	path of player
	dribble
	screen
	block
	rear turn
	pivot
	shot

1

coaching principles
and philosophies

General perspective

Basketball is only a part of the general educational system and must be kept in its proper perspective. A coach should familiarize himself with the administrative policies and regulations of the school and follow them to the letter with a cooperative and cordial attitude. He should cooperate fully with the eligibility and scholarship regulations of the school and conference and support them 100 per cent.

Faculty standing

The coach is a member of the faculty and must endeavor to follow the approved methods and techniques of ethical and efficient teaching. He must conduct himself with dignity and be fully aware of his responsibilities as a leader of youth.

Training and health

The health of the players is of supreme importance. A careful training program must be outlined and every possible measure taken to protect the squad. An injured player should never be neglected by the coach. Nor should the injured player be encouraged or forced to play without being thoroughly examined and declared fit by the school physician. The coach must never forget that he is not a physician. He should, therefore, refrain from prescribing treatment for illnesses or injuries.

School loyalty

It is important that the coach make a special effort to be liked and respected by the student body, the faculty, the administration, fellow coaches, and players. He should attend all pep meetings and boost his coaching associates and their teams. The intramural program should be respected and the coach should give it his full support, since it is an important part of the over-all program.

Public relations

The coach should become acquainted with the townspeople, parents, and all phases of the life of the community. His relationship with the parents of the team members should be warm and friendly. The coach is concerned with their most vital interests. Further, the youngsters are at an impressionable age and the parents are vitally interested in their welfare and progress. It is wise to remember that success is not wholly determined by the winning of games.

Publicity

The student paper and the local newspaper are vital assets. The coach should see that they get plenty of material to use in publicizing his sport. He should see that the games are announced and written up. He should be frank with newspaper friends but he should be extremely careful about chance remarks since they may be misinterpreted.

Sportsmanship

Since the building of character and sportsmanship is of major importance in sports, it is the duty of the coach to make sure that his actions and those of his players present high ideals of sportsmanship at all times and in all situations. The coach must remember that his own behavior and speech set a pattern for his players, spectators and other partisans. Going further, the coach should avoid "pouring it on" a weak team, criticizing another coach or an official, or humiliating anyone under any circumstance.

Rules

Without rules there can be no game. The coach must follow and abide by them and coach within the bounds of correct interpretations. The coach should also recognize the difficulties met in game officiating and do everything in his power to support the officials. If an official is clearly incompetent, he should be reported through the proper officials' organization.

Professional interest

The coach should be aware of his personal limitations with respect to complete knowledge of the game. He must, therefore, be a student of the game, trying constantly to improve his knowledge by reading pertinent texts, through graduate study, and by attending coaching schools, summer courses, and college and professional games.

The coach should do everything in his power to promote interest in the game, aid in the development of equipment, and safeguard the welfare of his players. He should endeavor to improve the game in his community in every way—for example, by sponsoring clinics and by inviting leading personalities of the game to visit his school.

It is vital that the coach study, analyze, and experiment with every aspect of the game. He should be enthusiastic, energetic, industrious, and work tirelessly to advance basketball.

One of the greatest aids to basketball coaching is attendance at a number of the coaching clinics held each year. I have gone to many clinics, I have lectured at a great many, and I have never failed to find something that could help me in my coaching while at St. John's, the University of North Carolina, the Philadelphia Warriors, and the University of South Carolina.

After we have been coaching a few years we tend to neglect certain phases of the game. However, when you attend coaching clinics many offensive and defensive techniques are brought back to mind. At all clinics in which I have lectured throughout the country I always outline the system that I have used over the years and with which I have been most successful; I do not attempt to present any style of play except my own.

Basically, my system of basketball stems from my background of basketball at St. John's University, Brooklyn, N. Y., and the Visitation Triangles which was a member of the old American Professional League. This is the background for the type of basketball I teach, and I might add that I have always placed more stress on defensive basketball than on the offensive game.

At the University of South Carolina we take movies of all of our home and tournament games. This is the most important impersonal item our coaching outline stresses. As soon as they are developed, we show the pictures to the players and check them again and again, pointing out the mistakes and then running through them on the basketball court.

At the beginning of the practice season, we take individual movies of each player in his execution of the fundamentals. These pictures enable us to check each player and apply corrective work as needed. The use of movies in coaching is still in its infancy, but in the future more and more coaches will take advantage of this valuable coaching item. Still camera shots can also be used to check form and execution of the fundamentals.

Player-coach relationship

The coach should be friendly with his players and strive to develop mutual respect and confidence. He should check their mistakes but be understanding of their failures. Perhaps the failure can be attributed to a teaching weakness. The coach should be understanding, sympathetic, and yet firm in dealing with his players. In his coaching he should be exacting, but quick to praise.

A list of training rules is important. Once initiated, the rules must be enforced. The coach must impress his players with the importance of study and with their duty to parents, the team, and their school to maintain academic standing and eligibility.

The team

The coach must coordinate the individual players of his squad into a team of which each is an important part. He should inspire his players to love the game and instill the desire to win. The coach should be with his team after every game—win or lose. Especially in defeat should he stand beside them, sharing their disappointment, but lifting their spirits by his confidence in the future.

Fundamentals

The sound approach to coaching begins with the teaching of fundamentals. The coach must have the patience to drill and drill and drill again in the correct performance of the fundamental skills of the game. There is no short-cut to successful coaching. Trick methods, short-cuts, and Fancy Dan plays lead only to disaster. A good team is one that is sound—fundamentally!

Leadership

The coach must have the ability to take charge, since he can develop leadership in his players only by displaying confidence, poise, and aggressiveness in a given situation. Action of some kind in a crisis is better than no action at all.

Practice programs

The coach should plan his season and his daily practices carefully since time is precious. Without careful planning it is easy to overlook an important part of the program. Yet, while following through with intelligent and careful planning and a driving, game-type workout, the coach must not forget the importance of "fun" in his practices.

Since the coach must conserve every minute of his practice time, he should demand that the players report promptly for the workouts and games. Supervision of the locker room is important to control horseplay and to check injuries. The coach and his assistants, managers, trainers, and other leaders should set the example.

Planned practice sessions conserve time and aid in sustaining attention. There should be such complete understanding between the coach and the players that his voice or a blast on the whistle will command immediate attention.

It has been said time and again that basketball is a game of habits. The down-to-earth approach to the mastery of fundamentals requires constant repetition through drills. However, the daily program should be planned so that each difficult and trying drill is followed by a "rest" or fun drill. This aids the coach in keeping his players alert and enthusiastic.

Repetition until the act becomes a habit is unquestionably the secret in mastering basketball skills. But such repetition without frequent change can and does develop player fatigue and monotony. A short, snappy drill on one phase of the game executed enthusiastically and then shifted to another and different type of work will insure much greater results.

Every drill in the coach's program should be directed specifically toward the development and improvement of a skill that blends into his planned offense and defense. Great teams are found to be composed of players who are strong in the execution of fundamentals.

Progress in learning, condition, and team spirit accompanied by a close personal relationship between coach and player will build strong *esprit de corps*. Discipline is necessary, but it can be developed more effectively through player respect than through position authority. It is wise, too, to keep in mind that harsh criticism destroys respect and confidence, whereas praise builds personal and team morale.

I like to come to each of my practices with something new. Perhaps it is a funny story, a new drill, a new play, or some sort of basketball idea that may prove a diversion from the usual practice work.

I believe in the value of individual coaching. A good way to work this into the practice program is to arrive early on the court and to move from one player to another and assist each with some phase of the game in which he needs help. I believe also in the value of working with small groups. Long lines of players who must wait interminably a turn in executing a drill means a poorly organized practice program and the loss of valuable working time. Form your players into small groups at different locations on the floor and see that every player is kept busy.

College basketball practice is restricted until October 15 of each year. To help players get in shape it is suggested that they go out for the cross country team. This training program usually runs from the second week of school to the opening day of basketball practice. Players who cannot avail themselves of cross country training can work out on their own in three-man basketball games.

In order to attain good conditioning of the legs and feet and to avoid shin splints and blisters one must be ready to go as soon as regular basketball practice starts. Pre-season practice in running, playing three-man basketball, and rope skipping will help condition the legs for the hard running so necessary in playing good basketball.

Since the days when I watched the great fighters train near my home in Greenwood Lake, N. Y., I have been intrigued by the value of rope skipping. This exercise helps increase jumping ability and the running and skipping moves in basketball. Rope skipping also develops the wrists and helps the basketball player develop the fluid movement so important in dribbling and shooting.

A program of isometric exercises is recommended for those players who appear in need of physical development. The program is set up on the basis of five days per week before and after the actual basketball season. Once the season is under way, the players are expected to continue the program twice weekly on their own. Space does not permit presentation of the complete program which stresses the following: press; arm pull; leg press; shins support; hamstrings; groin; curl; hand and wrist towel squeeze; arm-hand with frog kick.

The coach

The coach is much more than a teacher of sports. He is a leader of youth. Cleanliness of mind, person, dress, and speech are as much a part of his stock in trade as a knowledge of basketball. And, since the players represent the school, the community, and the coach, it is important that they be taught the value of personal cleanliness, clean and well-pressed clothing, politeness, courtesy, clean speech, and good table manners. Furthermore, since their schoolmates often use them as examples, they should not permit themselves to become sloppy in dress or to go unshaven, or the like. The coach must demand that the players observe the same rigid self-discipline he observes.

Boys and young men are highly impressionable, particularly in the field of sports. Quite often, whether he realizes it or not, the coach becomes a sort of hero to his players and other youngsters. It is imperative that he make a wholesome impact, demonstrate manliness, a strong competitive spirit, exemplify good sportsmanship, and stress strict observance of the rules. All coaches teach character—and their degree of success is in no way measured by games won or lost.

Most important of all, the coach must remember that he represents the type of man to whom he would entrust his own son for character training.

MY BASKETBALL PHILOSOPHY

One definition of a philosophy is that it is one's personal attitude expressed in a systematic body of general conceptions with the implication that they will be generally applied.

It sounds pretty involved to me, but I try to follow a philosophy with the game of basketball that may be reflected in the following paragraphs.

The player

It is my belief that all of basketball starts, continues, and ends with the player. I believe that it is my job to instill spirit and enthusiasm in my players, inspire them with the intense desire to be the best players in the world, and imbue them with a winning spirit.

I believe that it is important to pour it on my players and make them work hard. I also believe that it is my job to so convince them that hard work pays great individual and team dividends that they will *want* to work hard. Along this line, I believe that a player remembers and respects most the coach who drills him hard and, through repetition, makes him do it right.

Happy players are good players. Practices and games should be fun. Too much work and too little fun results in boredom and staleness. I like to plan my practices so they will not become monotonous. To that end, I like to keep the workouts hopping, shifting rapidly from one drill to another, accompanied by a lot of good-natured yelling and player enthusiasm.

Though it is important to have player discipline in order to get the best out of a boy, I want him to understand that it is *he* who plays the game, not the coach. And I want him to play freely, without fear of making a mistake. Only in free play can a boy respond spontaneously to game situations.

It is easy to overplay the important members of the team. It is easy to do them an injustice by keeping them in the game in order to build up an impressive score or to increase an individual scoring record. Keep in mind that fatigue increases and player effectiveness decreases with the amount of time played.

I like to have a good supporting cast for my first five and to make the seconds feel important. I realize that reserves will never develop poise and confidence unless they are used in regular game play. And I realize, too, that they will never feel they really belong unless they are used in the games. Using reserves for varsity "fodder" results in disgruntled players who can easily influence regulars in the wrong way of thinking. My players and everyone concerned must feel that the team is greater than the star, greater than the first five, the coach, or any other individual. In addition to bringing my varsity reserves along, I pay particular attention to the freshmen and the jayvee players and make sure that they realize that I am sincerely interested in their progress.

Lastly, I must feel that every player who plays for me takes something more than basketball skills and game experiences with him when he graduates.

The team

I believe that morale, poise, skill, confidence, and the will to win are vitally important. Team intelligence and the ability to take advantage of game opportunities are necessary for championship play. An important part of my job is to impress my players that, in most cases, the team that makes the fewest mistakes will win.

I feel it is my responsibility to see that my team is equipped with a basic attack to meet man-to-man and zone defenses and that it can use variations and modifications to take care of special situations. Naturally, the team should have the ability to change its style of play a number of times so that an effective attack can be summoned in any emergency. To that end, my team should and must have team adaptability.

TEAM ADAPTABILITY

1. *Slow down the offense when an opponent is too fast.*

2. *Crash the offensive board if the opponents cannot fast-break.*

3. *Play a possession game when the opponents adopt that style of play (meet fire with fire).*

4. *Use the stall offense when the opponents have an unusually tall defensive player who can block our close-to-the-basket shots (maneuver him out of position with a planned attack).*

5. *Utilize the fast break when the opponents do not observe defensive balance or are big and slow.*

Finally, I demand that my players be conditioned and prepared to put pressure on the opponents all the way—throughout the game, down the stretch, and in the overtime periods. This is possible only when every player is in tip-top shape and remains that way from the first game of the season to the last.

Coaching

I believe the coach must exude tremendous enthusiasm for the game. He must love the sport and be willing to give freely of every part of his being to the game. He must believe in himself and in his methods and techniques; he must keep constantly in mind that basketball is a game of fundamentals. Above all, *he must be himself.*

I think every coach should have a predetermined concept of his style of attack and that he should drill his players in his methods until they become second nature. However, it is important to remember that it is easy to "overcoach."

Mimeographed copies of attacks and game situations are easy to prepare and are great coaching aids. I like to hold frequent skull practices and use the blackboard and the strategy board to illustrate situations. In this connection, I believe it is important that the player take a leading part in explaining the purposes and reasons for the pertinent offenses in the given situations.

Time is of the essence; wasted time is dangerous. Each of my practices is outlined, and the outline is followed at full speed. Short practices, during which the elements are run off smoothly and enthusiastically, are much more valuable than long-drawn-out workouts.

I believe in stressing a philosophy of pressure offense. I feel it is important that my players feel that they are champions, that the opponents must worry about *us.*

I am fully aware that the health of my players is vital. Therefore, it is important that they be protected from colds, sprains, foot blisters, and other threats. Here the services of a trainer or a team physician are invaluable. Training rules should require a certain amount of sleep, regular meals, and other sound practices as outlined later on in this chapter.

I believe that my team must be well trained in the basic skills. Every player should be a good shooter, have basketball speed, be well conditioned, be an expert ball handler, know the importance of offensive rebounding, and understand the basic offenses and their application.

The coach should have a close relationship with his captain and his quarterback. Daily talks and a "meeting of the minds" with respect to strategy and game tactics are important.

I try to use all my players. I like to get my substitutes into the game when we have a lead and/or in the first half of any game. No game is ever lost in the first half. It is important that my best five be ready for the final part of the game—rested, free from the worry of personal fouls, and in a good competitive frame of mind.

Every game is THE game. You invite disaster when you look ahead to a future rival and forget the game at hand. It is far better to try to win them "one at a time."

Practices

I believe that practice sessions should simulate game conditions as closely as possible. Since our games at South Carolina University are usually played at night, I favor night practices. (I realize that this may not be possible in high-school and preparatory-school competition for many reasons that usually do not affect college coaching.) I believe in charted areas and spots for shooting, and I believe that players shoot better from certain areas on the court than from others.

The offense

In my opinion, team offense begins with the fast break. But I also believe that it should be a controlled break and one that lends itself to the best use of the player talent available. I like my players to be so skilled in the use of the fast break that they can pull out of it without a bad shot or loss of the ball when it is obvious that the advantage is lost.

I do not believe in a set offense or in set plays as such. In my opinion, any offense is good that employs free circulation, floor balance, and coordination of the players through the execution of fundamentals. However, in teaching my type of offense, I believe in drilling my players in certain plays and series of plays in order to develop automatic passing and scoring reactions to the situations that may be met.

I believe in slowing down my team's attack when I feel it is necessary in order to win. And I believe in freezing the ball when it may insure victory.

I believe that it is extremely important to make definite plans and practice regularly getting the ball from the center jump, from held balls, loose balls, and rebounds, and through interceptions.

Offensively, it is a coach's responsibility to see that his team is equipped for the following game situations:

OFFENSE CHECKLIST

1. To control or steal the tap

2. Jump-ball plays

3. Out-of-bounds plays

4. The fast break

5. The single-pivot offense

6. The single-post offense

7. A spread offense (center kept open)

8. Crash the offensive backboard

9. Possession of the ball (the stall)

10. Freeze the ball

11. Meet the press (man-to-man and zone)
    Semi-press
    Half-court press
    Full press

12. Beat the sag and float

13. Attack the man-to-man variations

14. Penetrate the zones

The defense

Defense was my playing forte. I have, therefore, stressed team defense in my coaching. I believe a team should be equipped to counter every offensive move which might be encountered during the season. Defensive plans should be made prior to the first practice and based on the defensive abilities of the returning players. Unlike football, a coach cannot send in a defensive platoon to meet the opposing team's offense. Therefore, his team must be thoroughly prepared in advance to meet any and all possible offenses. I would like to add here that the team should not only be prepared to meet the various offenses in the practice workouts but given game experience if only for two or three minutes. Game experience will give the players confidence and enable the coach to detect flaws in the execution of the defense.

Being a New Yorker, my concept of defense has always been based upon the straight man-to-man type. Through the years, however, certain offenses began to overpower the straight man-to-man and I began to experiment with the variations—overshifting, sagging, floating, playing in front of the big man, and so on. Later, I found that it was necessary to prepare my teams to meet the opponents' fast break, possession game, expert screening attack, big-man threat (often two or three big men), freeze and all types of press applications, and situation plays (center jump, held ball, free-throw, one shot, and out-of-bounds plays).

The game

The coach should have his team ready to adapt an offense to meet any defense, and he must not be afraid to gamble. He should make the decisions. The players expect him to lead and to take the initiative when decisions are necessary. He should not sit and wait and hope that things will improve. He should act!

PLANNING THE SEASON

Pre-season

A coach should keep in close touch with his players during the entire year. Most boys who play basketball become specialists in the sport and play the year around. Year-round play is possible because of the development of summer basketball and the construction of outdoor courts all over the country. The veteran member of the team may not need much advice toward improving himself during the summer, but the freshmen and other players who have not reached a high degree of development should be given some suggestions so that they may work on them during the summer. Mere thinking about these suggestions will help, and the fact that the coach has given thought to their improvement is important in building the players' morale.

When it is impossible to keep in close personal contact with his players, the coach can send them a general letter a month or six weeks previous to the opening practice. This letter should contain an outline of the season plans and objectives and some personal hints for individual improvement, as well as some suggestions concerning conditioning. It is wise to advise the player that he should *not* engage in regular games prior to the first practice, but that he should shoot around for fun, improve his dribbling, passing, rebounding, jumping, and other fundamentals. Certain exercises such as rope skipping, light calisthenics, shadow boxing, use of a medicine ball, and running to strengthen the legs and improve the wind are to be recommended.

Gymnasium and equipment

The head coach should personally check the equipment he will need for the season, making sure that it is in good condition and that there is sufficient quantity to adequately suit-up his varsity, junior varsity, freshmen, and other teams. Next he should inspect the gymnasium to see that the court is well marked and in good condition. The baskets, nets, scoreboard, time clock, and scoring tables should also be checked at this time.

The captain

The selection of a captain is a serious matter for everyone concerned: the school, the student body, the coach, and particularly the team. Since the captain is the team's representative, I want to be sure the right man is selected. For some years I have personally appointed the captain and the method has been successful.

Managers

A good senior manager means a good start. It is important that the right youngster have the job. It has been my good fortune to have managers who were fine administrators and enthusiastic sportsmen.

An organization functioning year after year in which freshmen, sophomores, juniors, and seniors advance in that order to the position of head manager means that the coach will have an experienced and interested youngster on hand to handle the hundred and one details and responsibilities encountered during the season.

The duties are too numerous to discuss here. However, if a check list is mimeographed for each practice, home game, game away from home, and tournament, it will eliminate many oversights and insure the proper execution of the managers' duties.

Staff meetings

The head coach will undoubtedly have his season plans formulated in advance, but it is wise to devote several staff meetings to their discussion. The assistant coaches, trainer, captain, and senior manager should be present.

At these meetings the duties of each member of the staff should be outlined and, in general, the following should be discussed:

MEETING CHECK LIST

1. *Review the previous season's highlights, weaknesses of the team such as shooting, ball handling, defense, use of the fast break, rebounding, blocking out, taking bad shots, condition, cliques, spirit.*

2. *Evaluate returning and new players.*

3. *Plan the offense and defense.*

4. *Set up conditioning and training rules.*

5. *Plan the use of teaching aids, movies, charts.*

6. *Plan a practice outline built around the season's schedule.*

7. *Discuss drills and special attacks and defenses.*

8. *Prepare player progress charts, game performance charts.*

9. *Plan for trips and look ahead to tournaments.*

Squad meetings

Several orientation meetings should precede actual floor practices. With the liberal use of a blackboard, the coach can familiarize the squad with his offensive and defensive theories of the game, conditioning and training rules; outline and discuss his season plans, drills, and practice outlines; and cover the basketball rules.

Forms for physical examinations and parents' playing permission can be distributed and gotten out of the way. The entire staff should take part in these meetings and cover their assigned duties so that all concerned will understand their responsibilities.

Conditioning

Pre-season work by the individual player should enable him to report for the early-season practices in fairly good condition. If a new candidate or even a veteran is not sufficiently interested in his personal physical condition to do some pre-season work, it is doubtful that he will contribute much to the team. Personally, I find that it is impossible to keep my players away from basketball. Many of them work out all summer and, as soon as school opens, they are at it again—practicing their shots, dribbling, driving-in, rebounding, passing. This means that I can begin my early-season work fairly certain that much of the basic conditioning has been completed.

I believe that conditioning can be most wisely accomplished through basic drills and training in fundamentals. However, calisthenics, rope skipping, shadow boxing, and the use of medicine balls are excellent conditioners. Medicine-ball drills are excellent for loosening up the fingers, strengthening wrists, and for practicing all passes. Incorporating bending, turning, and twisting insures a good workout before actual practice begins.

Early season (first two weeks of practice)

The consideration in early practice is the integration of conditioning activity with fundamental drills that are directed toward the development of basketball skills. For example, the development of leg power and "wind" can be accomplished just as easily by a fast-break drill or a full-press drill as by running on an outdoor track.

A word of caution is advisable here. The feet are unused to the hard running and the sudden stops and starts, and it is wise to limit such action for the first few days. The use of two pairs of sox and a commercial hardening application will be of great help. Tincture of Benzoin will harden the skin, assist in preventing blisters, and prevent athlete's foot.

Many coaches jeopardize the entire season by overworking their players during the first few practices. It is easy to work your players so hard the first day or two that they may be crippled for an entire week. This means loss of time and, more important, loss of the player. Naturally, the conditioning program is stepped up until the squad is able to work at full speed during the entire practice session.

The players soon become familiar with the coaching methods, and now a time schedule can be put into operation. I work no more than five or ten minutes on a single fundamental or drill. Midway in the practice I like to allow a ten-minute freedom "break" in which the players may do as they wish.

In season

Once the game season arrives, the big problem is to maintain the conditioning level achieved in the early-season workouts. This can be a serious problem because of the time required for special offensive and defensive work in preparing for the next opponent, light practices following and preceding difficult games, and in travel.

We limit our daily in-season practices to one and one-half hours. It is felt that this amount of time is sufficient. It is easy to lose a game by over-work on the practice court. Following the first game at home we will practice the next day as follows:

DRESSING ROOM MEETING   3:00 p.m.
    Check previous game's mistakes
    Check movies of game
PRACTICE COURT   4:00 p.m.
    Warmup drills
    Next game offense
    Next game defense
    On-floor application of scouting information

The second day we step up the program as follows:

1. Rope skipping (five minutes)
2. Medicine ball work
3. Isometric drills
4. Three-man criss-cross drill
5. Fast-break run
6. Lay-ups on both sides of basket and down the middle
7. Defensive drills (stance, slide, hands, talk)
8. Offensive practice
9. Team defenses (presses, zones)
10. Game type scrimmage with new offense
11. Freezing ball techniques
12. Simulated game situations

Training rules

The trainer is an invaluable member of the staff. His advice in setting up the practice outlines, establishing the training rules, and determining a proper and balanced diet is followed to the letter. Naturally, the high school coach must, in most cases, assume this responsibility with the assistance of the school physician.

GENERAL. I have never drawn up a definite set of training rules. I believe that the players should be aware of the importance of securing plenty of sleep, a balanced diet, an abundance of fruit, and plenty of water between meals. Naturally, smoking and the use of intoxicating beverages cannot be countenanced.

A basketball player acquires drive through hard training, forcing himself day after day beyond the point at which he first becomes fatigued until he reaches his maximum potential. For that reason, I do not believe in lay-offs during the season. If practices are interrupted for any reason, I believe the player should be urged to keep in shape through roadwork, calisthenics, volleyball, and the like.

If the players desire a good team and are sold on training as vital to the success of the team, they will be glad to cooperate. It is fairly easy to tell whether training rules are being violated. Inability to keep up with teammates in the usual drills, poor condition, nervousness, and fatigue are indications.

WEIGHT PROBLEMS. A weight chart should be kept by the trainer, assistant coach, or manager. The player should weigh-in for practice and weigh-out after his shower. A study of the chart from time to time will enable the trainer or coach to determine whether the player is losing weight too rapidly. If so, it is wise to have the boy checked by a physician. After the first two or three weeks the athlete who maintains his weight level certainly is not overtrained and is in little danger of going stale.

SLEEP. The highly trained and conditioned basketball player requires from eight to ten hours of sleep. During sleep the body repairs broken-down tissue, renews muscular strength, and disposes of waste products.

DIET. The subject of diet for the athlete has been controversial for many years. However, it is certain that three regular meals a day are necessary. Breakfast and dinner should be heavy meals and lunch should be light.

The player should not practice for at least two hours after meals, nor should he eat for at least an hour after practice. Before games it is wise to eat three to four hours before the contest. It is my opinion that a normal mixed diet is sufficient for the average athlete.

The college coach has the assistance of an efficient trainer and usually a training table under the direction of a trained dietician. This normally takes care of the problem. The high school coach must rely upon the athlete's parents. The average mother normally prepares meals that are appetizing, appealing to the eye, and well balanced. She will usually be glad to follow the suggestions of the coach with respect to diet in the interests of her son.

Something like the following might be suggested to the player's mother:

BREAKFAST

Fruit juice

Whole fruit (such as grapefruit, oranges, pears)

Cereal (whole grain)

Eggs (poached, boiled, scrambled)

Ham or bacon (small portion)

Toast and jelly

Milk

LUNCH

Soup

Sandwich

Salad

Fresh fruit

Toast

Milk or tea

DINNER

Lean meat, fowl, or fish

Fresh vegetables (raw)

Cooked vegetables

Dessert

Toast

Milk

PRE-GAME MEAL

12-ounce steak

Baked potato

Dry toast

Fruit cup

Hot tea

or

Poached egg

Thin slice of beef (no gravy)

Fruit juices

Toast

Moderate cool water

Tea

Something sweet (chocolate bar)

2

building a style of play

The Two-Three

In my opinion the "Two-Three" offense is the best in basketball. It blends in perfectly with the give-and-go (Eastern) type of play with which I am most familiar. It can cope with straight, loose, tight, sag and floating man-to-man; switching; man-to-man and zone presses, and/or the zone defenses.

All professional teams use the Two-Three chiefly because it permits extensive use of the big man. All of the teams I have coached were built around a big man, since this was the starting point for all coaches in the East and was the dominant feature of practically all of the teams I came in contact with during my playing and coaching days.

The Two-Three offense is flexible enough in attacking the man-to-man, switching and combination defenses to permit the use of the One-Two-Two, the five-man give-and-go weave, the four-man weave with a post or pivot, the five-man roll, and approaches closely enough to the Three-Two offense for purposes of this book.

We combine the above formations in the development of our man-to-man offense at South Carolina. Basically, the formation (Two-Three)

19

is designed to permit free-lance play from a set formation. At South Carolina we feature the one-on-one, two-on-two, and three-man plays.

No coach will succeed with an offensive pattern or style unless his players have both a complete knowledge of the fundamentals and the ability to put them into practice under game conditions. It follows, then, that players will not be able to successfully employ a style of play unless they have been exposed to fundamental drills time after time until the use of the correct fundamentals in the various situations has become a habit.

The five-man give-and-go weave, the use of inside, outside, moving and stop screens, big men in the single or double pivot and/or post, the five-man roll and the four-man roll with a post, pivot or both all have a place in the Two-Three offense.

The basic One-Three-One attack for use against the zone defenses will be diagrammed and explained. Naturally, all coaches have their own theories and adaptations for use against a particular type of zone and its variations.

It is important to reiterate that the use of a pattern, weave, or roll is vital in any basic offense in order to insure offensive and defensive balance. Otherwise, the development of game plays has little value except to teach situation reactions.

The charts do not show scoring attempts by the players since all offensive players are operating with complete option freedom in all plays. The players are, however, expected to follow the regular or reverse circulation paths. Frequently a player will cut in an entirely different direction from the required circulation and then change his path to end up correctly in the proper continuity.

The post-pivot player is used as a scoring threat in all formations, although none of the diagrams show him attempting a shot. In his capacity as a blocker or post or pivot player he has many opportunities to handle the ball and may elect to fake a hand-off and attempt a shot whenever he feels it is the correct option.

ADVANCING THE BALL

Advancing the ball to the front court is not as simple as it may appear. Not infrequently a game is lost or an important basket is scored through an interception on the pass-in from out-of-bounds under the opponents' basket. Following a score, a player of the team that has just scored the basket may play "dummy" and start upcourt. Then, with perfect timing, he will turn and make the interception. An easy two points usually follow. This interception is usually made because the player taking the ball out of bounds makes a hurried or careless pass to a teammate, disregarding the nearby opponent.

Advance opportunities follow interceptions, recovery of loose balls, rebounds, held balls, out-of-bounds plays, a scoring shot from the field, or following a successful or unsuccessful free throw.

Surprise defensive moves are the rule rather than the exception in basketball as it is played today. Many of these surprise defenses are applied before the ball crosses the ten-second line. Today, the press or some other form of a forcing defense is used at one time or another in practically every game played.

The advance following an interception, recovery of a loose ball, or a "deep" rebound is made so quickly that the opponents usually forget everything except speeding for their defensive positions at the other end of the court. Under these conditions, use of the press or some other form of a forcing defense is impossible. However, following a free throw, successful or not, an out-of-bounds play, a successful shot from the field, jump-ball situations, and most short rebounds—some sort of the press is possible.

If the opponents are behind in the score, such surprise tactics are to be expected. Most assuredly the well-coached team should be prepared to meet these defensive moves.

Front-line players often break upcourt to reach their attack positions immediately after a score. Quite often, too, they turn their backs and leave the backcourt players to bring the ball upcourt as best they can. Here, a careless dribbler may fall for an opponent's dummy play and a sudden attack may result in loss of the ball. In some cases the two backcourt players may pass the ball back and forth while advancing upcourt and be unprepared for a sudden defensive move.

The coach must make sure that his team is prepared to meet any and all of these surprise moves in the slow advance. Front-line players must be coached to advance with their eyes focused on their backcourt teammates, prepared to break back toward the ball should help be needed.

The player taking the ball out of bounds following a score should always watch nearby opponents and use a fake before releasing the ball. Dribblers should protect the ball by dribbling more slowly and carefully, making sure that a teammate is near at hand should a sudden pass be necessary. If two backcourt players are passing the ball back and forth while advancing, they should make sure their passes do not take them too close to opponents.

When scouting notes or bitter game experiences warn a team that the opponents use these surprise moves, three men may be assigned to bring the ball upcourt in the slow advance. These players may use screening tactics for the advance, weaving and cutting from side to side to protect the ball.

THE FAST BREAK

The fast break is the most important offensive system in basketball. It is used by practically every coach in the game, and its effectiveness is usually determined by the amount of time spent in developing and exploring its possibilities. The chief objective is to advance the ball into a scoring area before the opponents have a chance to get into defensive position. Second in importance is the outnumbering of the defensive opponents so that an attacking player may secure an unguarded shot.

Efficient use of the fast break results in numerous easy and quick scores which often demoralize a good team. The fast break is colorful, full of sparkling plays, and a sure crowd-pleaser. All players enjoy the action because of the speed and dash with which it is executed.

Some coaches advocate the use of a weave in the break down the floor. Others operate on the theory that a straight line is the shortest distance between two points and advance their players in straight lines. One coach advocates the use of the short pass while others feature the long pass. Another coach attempts to eliminate the dribble, and still another believes it is the best and safest method possible to advance the ball.

Some teams employ the "press" during the entire game, and it may well be said that their offense is a consistent and continuous use of the fast break. However, these teams are in the minority; the majority of coaches believe in combining use of the fast break with a set or formal offense.

The fast break is a team offense. It lends itself to innumerable plays and can be used following every recovery of the ball. I believe in a controlled fast break with an emphasis on short passes. If the fast break is to be most effective, the team must be aggressive and prepared to take chances. Since it is important to get down the floor as quickly as possible, certain players often break before their team gains possession of the ball. In a number of instances a teammate may be in an uncontested position to secure possession of the ball and the quick dash downcourt may result in a long, successful pass and an easy basket.

The fast break from a man-to-man defense differs greatly from the break from a zone defense. In fact, many coaches feel that the positioning of the chasers and the rebounders and the ease with which a fast break may be initiated are the determining factors in recommending the use of the zone as the basic defense. Since the zone players have assigned areas (even when shifting), the rebounder can easily locate a receiver for his outlet pass. Further, use of the zone enables the coach to place good rebounders near the basket and the fast cutters in fast-break positions.

The long pass is the most difficult pass in the game. Some players never master the control necessary to use it accurately, and many players have difficulty in catching the speeding ball. Further, the long, diagonal outlet pass lends itself to more interception opportunities than the short pass. A long pass should not be made to a teammate unless he is all alone or there is plenty of daylight around him.

The dribble is of great value in the fast break because it limits, to a certain extent, bad passes and fumble possibilities. In certain situations the dribble is the best weapon to use in avoiding interception attempts. In addition, the use of the dribble in the center lane after the front court is reached places the ball in the middle of the floor and gives the outside-lane cutters more freedom in maneuvering for good shooting positions.

In some fast breaks, teammates in the outside lanes wait until the receiver of the outlet pass gets the ball before advancing downcourt. This spreads the breaking players across the court in a straight line and, of course, insures better passing. In other usage of the fast break the players make every attempt to get ahead of the ball. They drive for their basket immediately, filling the closest lane. Properly used, this is not a haphazard advance. The man with the ball is able to speed the advance since he has receivers ahead to whom he can pass. The players out in front of the ball are moving in predetermined paths and expect the ball. If they are advancing properly, one of the "sweepers" will usually be in a good position to receive the pass.

The following principles are recommended.

FAST-BREAK PRINCIPLES

1. *Every player on the defense should be fast-break conscious. He should be aware of his rebounding and lane responsibilities should a fast-break opportunity present itself, and he should immediately execute his move.*

2. *Fast breaks develop out of fumbles, interceptions, loose balls, backboard rebounds, successful and unsuccessful field and free-throw attempts, jump balls, and out-of-bounds situations. Naturally, the break starts from the point at which the ball is recovered. The players should be so schooled in the method of advance and the techniques of the particular fast break*

required that they react from any of the above situations without the slightest hesitation.

3. Since the majority of fast breaks develop from rebounds, securing the ball is of vital importance. Following a shot, all defensive players should first get position between their opponents and the basket. After a good blocking-out position is obtained, the defensive player divides his attention between his opponent and the direction of the rebound. When the direction of the rebound has been clearly determined, the player may leave his opponent to catch the ball.

All too frequently, when a shot is taken, a defensive player in a good blocking position will turn away from his opponent and hazard a guess at the direction of the rebound. Should a deep rebound result or should the ball be deflected in another direction, his opponent may make the recovery simply because he has not been properly blocked away from the basket.

4. The rebounder should get the outlet pass away quickly and safely. He should then back up the pass in case there is an interception or a fumble.

5. Filling the fast-break lanes should be initiated as soon as the ball is safely in the hands of the rebounder. The players nearest the sidelines should fill the outside lanes. They should move laterally and in such manner that they can see the ball. Before reaching the sidelines they should turn inward and be prepared for a pass should the rebounder so elect.

The player who normally fills the middle lane should be given the opportunity. However, if he is the rebounder, or is in a poor position, another player should fill the lane and fulfill the necessary requirements.

6. Following the outlet pass, all others should be short and fast. The dribble should be eliminated unless the player is caught in a poor passing position and must dribble to avoid travelling. In some situations the player is forced to dribble because potential receivers are covered. The three players in the first wave should continue downcourt on straight lines, passing the ball from side to side until the front court is reached. By this time, the scoring possibilities are evident. A three-on-two or even a three-on-one situation may be present.

7. As soon as the possible scoring situation is evident, the players should maneuver for the open shot. If the player driving down the center lane has been able to get the ball as he reaches the

outer half of the free-throw circle, he should stop just short of the free-throw line and prepare to attempt a shot. If a defensive opponent attempts to stop the shot, one of the outside-lane sweepers will be free for the pass and should have a clear shot.

Charts 2–5 show, in some part, the use of the fast break from certain game situations. Space does not permit presenting all the situations from which a fast break originates, but the principles used are effective in the great majority of fast-break opportunities.

The inside rebound area (see Chart 1) is to be filled with the expert rebounders when possible. They fill the spaces under the basket until they form a triangle. These positions should be obtained only after they have blocked their opponents away from the basket. In this connection, many tall rebounders develop the ability to retrieve the ball at the height of their leap, twist in the air, and fire an outlet pass accurately before hitting the floor. The hook pass is usually employed in this "in-the-air" pass.

The safety area for rebounders is located just outside the inside rebound area and is used only when the rebounder cannot get the ball away. He may dribble to this safety area or pass the ball to a teammate in the area. Rebounders are frequently guarded so closely that they cannot make an immediate outlet pass. In this situation the rebounder may whirl suddenly and dribble out of the rebound area and downcourt before passing.

The short-pass area begins at the free-throw line and extends three feet beyond the edge of the outer half of the free-throw circle. The majority of outlet passes are directed to receivers in this area. Some fast-break styles concentrate on a direct pass to a dribbler in the outer half of the free-throw circle after every rebound. The receiver then dribbles down the center lane while his teammates fill the outside lanes. It is a conservative and highly effective fast break and eliminates much of the danger of bad passes, interceptions, and fumbles found in the passing game.

Most coaches feel that it is important to fill the area near the free-throw line to prevent opponents from obtaining possible deep rebounds.

The long-pass area extends from the short-pass area to the ten-second line. Long passes should be thrown to teammates in this area only when they are completely free. Many outlet-pass interceptions occur in this area.

The cutting lanes extend from the short-pass area to the front-court baseline. The inside lane is the most direct to the goal. The small star in the center lane is placed near the spot where the dribbler or center man should begin to slow down so that he may safely stop short of

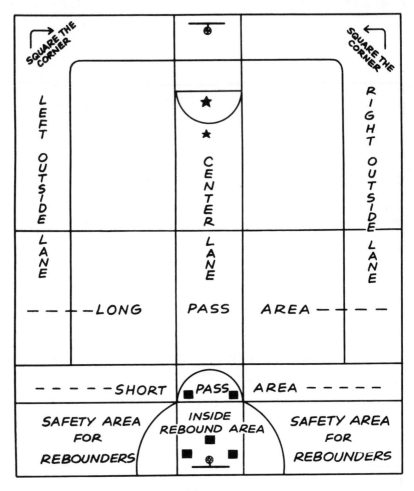

Chart 1

the free-throw line (large star). The right and left outside lanes extend to the baseline; teammates in this area should not expect the outlet pass unless they are completely free.

The angles in the front corners of the outside lanes are inserted to accentuate the importance of sweeping the corners and approaching the basket along the baseline (behind the defensive opponents).

Chart 2 shows the rebound in operation when a conservative fast-break style is used. Players *A*, *B*, and *C* are in the triangle formation under the basket. Players *D* and *E* have filled the outer half of the free-throw circle. When possession of the ball is assured, players *D* and *E* move laterally to the sidelines, crossing one another as shown to escape opponents if being pressed. In cutting toward the sidelines in this manner they place themselves in safer positions to receive a pass from the rebounders, since they are moving slightly toward the ball.

In Chart 2 the ball is being rebounded by player *B*, who passes on

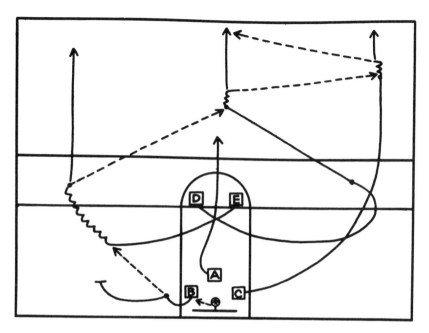

Chart 2

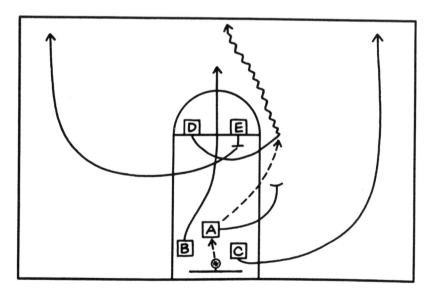

Chart 3

the same side to teammate *E* who is moving toward him. Player *E* dribbles until he is in the clear or until teammate *D* has reached the center lane. Then *E* passes to *D* and continues down the left lane. Player *D* may pass immediately to teammate *C* or dribble to get complete control of the ball before passing. Player *A* follows up the center lane as the "trailer." Note that rebounder *B* has followed the ball after passing to *E*.

The fast break shown in Chart 3 comes off a zone defense with the express purpose of getting the ball immediately to the outstanding dribbler and scorer (player *D*), who drives down the center of the court. A block may or may not be set by teammate *E*.

This type of fast break fills the lanes quickly and depends on the skill of the expert dribbler to advance the ball into scoring territory. The dribbler is always a dead shot from the free-throw line where he sets and shoots unless guarded. When guarded, he passes to one of the sweepers, or to the trailer.

Chart 4 shows the closing phase of the fast break. Player *D* has received the ball from teammate *C* and has slowed down to maintain a

Chart 4

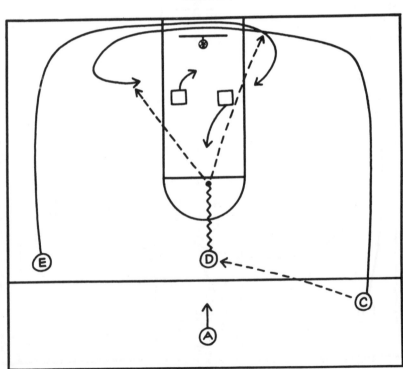

control dribble and to draw one of the two opponents out to guard him. Player *D* will stop short of the free-throw line prepared to shoot or to pass to sweepers *E* or *C*.

If dribbler *D* has difficulty in attempting a shot or passing to one of the sweepers, he will cut through the lane toward the basket. If a pass is made to the right or to the left, the trailer will cut on the side away from the receiver of the ball.

Note that players *E* and *C* have continued on under the basket and have circled back. This is shown because sweepers often outdistance the middle man and should do something to distract the opponents. Continuing on under the basket enables them to exchange positions and disturb the defensive players.

It is important that the center lane be filled by an expert dribbler who is also a good shot from the vicinity of the free-throw line. He should be a fine passer and able to fake a pass one way and feed the ball another. Frequently, he can leap in the air, fake a shot, and pass to the unguarded teammate. Bounce passes are, of course, imperative in this under-the-basket passing unless a teammate is completely free.

Chart 5 shows the fast break from an unsuccessful free throw. (Most unsuccessful free throws rebound to the right.) Rebounder *A* got the ball. As soon as players *B*, *C*, *D*, and *E* saw that teammate *A* made the rebound, they broke as shown.

Chart 5

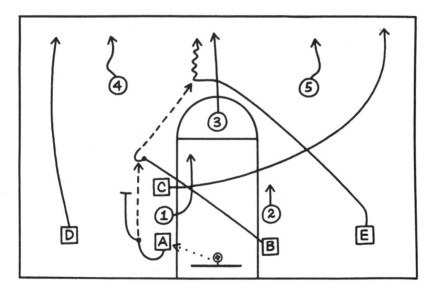

The takeoff path of player C should force backcourt opponent 5 to retreat to the defense. The dash down the left outside lane by player D should force player 4 to retreat, thus clearing the way for player A to make a good outlet pass to teammate B.

Player E should arrive at the center of the court in the center lane in time to receive the ball from teammate B; he can now pass or dribble the ball downcourt. Player C often beats the defense back and, if clear, may be hit with a long pass.

FAST-BREAK TIPS

1. *The rebounder should pass to a receiver on the same side of the court when possible.*

2. *Dribbling to the corner gives opponents time to retreat and set up their defense. Get the ball on its way as quickly as possible with a pass.*

3. *The pass to a teammate in an outside lane should be aimed at the outside shoulder so he may pivot away from an opponent who tries to intercept the ball.*

4. *Outside-lane cutters should get going. They should not wait for their center-lane teammate. Put the pressure on the opponent.*

5. *All passes except the outlet pass should be short. Don't attempt cross-court passes from one outside lane to the other.*

6. *If a cutter advances so far ahead of his teammates that a play is impossible, he should drive along the baseline to the other side of the court and circle back toward the basket on that side.*

7. *Don't be afraid to yell when you are free. And don't yell when you are not free.*

8. *Outside-lane cutters should avoid dribbling unless the teammate in the center lane is covered. Get the ball to the middle of the court when the front court is reached.*

9. *Keep spread in the drive down the court. Outside-lane sweepers must "square" the corners and continue along the baseline to the other side of the court if they are "ahead" of the play.*

10. *The middle man should dribble straight for the free-throw line and plan to stop there for a shot or a pass to an uncov-*

ered teammate. However, he should continue his drive when defensive opponents are out of position.

GIVE-AND-GO WEAVE

The give-and-go weave is the basic circulation used in the South Carolina University attack. The circulation may start from any point in the front court with a pass from the player in possession to his closest teammate. The passer then cuts directly down the lane and under the basket before turning toward the corner on the same side of the court as the teammate to whom he passed the ball. As the passer cuts for the basket he raises the hand away from the receiver high in the air as a target hand in case the receiver wishes to return the pass.

The receiver passes to the teammate on the opposite side of the court and also cuts down the middle with the opposite hand raised high. When he reaches the basket he cuts to the corner on the same side of the court as the player to whom he passed the ball.

The corner players replace the backcourt players and take their turns in receiving the ball, passing and cutting down the lane to the basket.

The give-and-go weave is an excellent medium for teaching passing, cutting, footwork, and teamwork, and in developing player condition. An important part of the give-and-go weave is the teaching of timing with relation to the execution of passes and player movement.

Most players like to execute the give-and-go weave at full speed, but it may easily be slowed down through the use of the dribble and passing up the next receiver. A change of pace in the use of this weave may be executed by reversing the direction of the pass.

The give-and-go weave lends itself to the use of inside and outside screens and, when incorporated with the dribble-block, change-ups, and moving posts and pivots, becomes a fine offense.

The weave can also be used to freeze the ball.

Charts 6 and 7 show the use of the weave with inside and outside screens.

Chart 6 shows use of the inside screen in the give-and-go weave. Player 1 passes the ball to teammate 2 and cuts between 2 and defensive opponent B (inside screen). He then cuts back toward the basket and, if he does not receive a return pass, fades right along the baseline to the right corner to maintain the continuity and to replace player 5.

After receiving the ball from teammate 1, player 2 fakes a return pass to him and then dribbles laterally across-court. Player 2 then passes to teammate 3, cuts in front of defensive opponent C (inside screen), and cuts for the basket. If he does not receive a return pass, he fades left along the baseline to the left corner to maintain the continuity and re-place player 4. The continuity is kept up in this manner with player 4 and player 5 replacing player 1 and player 2 and, in turn, using the in-side screen and cutting for the basket.

Chart 6

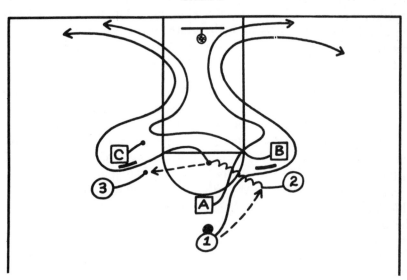

Chart 7

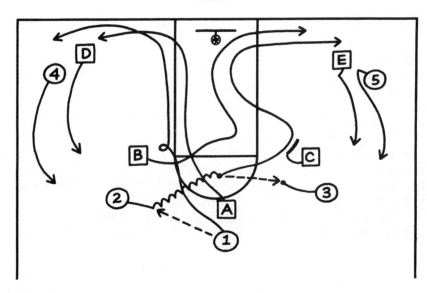

Chart 7 shows use of the outside screen in the give-and-go weave. Player 1 passes the ball to teammate 2 and cuts close behind defensive opponent *B* (outside screen). He then drives for the basket and fades left to the left corner to maintain the continuity and to replace teammate 4.

After receiving the ball from teammate 1, player 2 fakes a return pass to him, advances slightly with a dribble, and passes to teammate 3. He then cuts close behind defensive opponent *C* (outside screen) and drives for the basket. If he does not receive a return pass from teammate 3, player 2 fades right along the baseline to the right corner to maintain the continuity and to replace teammate 5. The continuity continues in this manner with player 4 and player 5 replacing teammate 1 and teammate 2 and, in turn, using the outside screen and cutting for the basket.

UTILIZING THE BIG MAN

I regard the big man as the key player in all of the South Carolina offenses. His development or education in the skills that may be utilized in the offense is vital to its success. Although the ability to score is important, it should not take precedence over the ability to play defense (block-out, switch, rebound) and to blend into the offense by handling the ball, getting the rebound outlet pass away, general screening, setting up blocking plays, cutting, and following in.

Naturally, such personal skills as shooting, faking, and feinting should be developed to the fullest extent. The fakes must include foot fakes and fakes with the hands and with the ball. The feints must include use of the head, eyes, and the body. Special stunts such as pitting the big fellow against a smaller man in one-on-one play will help in his development.

Rope skipping, bag punching, shadow boxing, dancing, "tap-in" drills, the day-after-day squeezing of a handball, and the use of a medicine ball for finger, wrist, and arm development—all are important.

Special practice in two-on-two play is valuable in the development of the big man since here he will learn the vital man-to-man defensive moves (front-slide-stay-switch) and fast, accurate passing and cutting.

The pivot player must learn through actual competition how to secure and hold position on his opponent. Many big fellows lack the timing sense necessary in obtaining position; they arrive too early or too late. Some big men master the timing requirements but lack the ability to handle the ball effectively when they receive it.

Among the most difficult qualities to teach the big man are poise and confidence. He must realize that he is the pivot around which the offense evolves. As soon as he is aware of this, he should be forced to take charge. He should signify by hand or other signals when he wants the ball and where he expects it to be thrown. His moves must be made with sureness and confidence.

The ability to pivot away, pivot back, cut under the basket and reverse back to the desired position is important in securing a good scoring position; this ability is acquired only by long hours of practice. The know-how necessary to fake a shot and drive around an opponent or to fake a dribble and take the shot, again, comes only after hard and patient work, as does the ability to set up blocks, posts and turnaround positions.

Chart 8 shows the give-and-go weave with post-pivot. Player 1 passes to teammate 2 and screens inside or outside. He then cuts directly down the lane for the basket and around and in back of pivot player 5. He continues along the baseline to the right corner to replace teammate 4.

After receiving the ball from teammate 1, player 2 dribbles to the left, passes to teammate 3, and cuts down the lane to and under the basket and along the baseline to the left corner.

Player 4 has now reached the backcourt. When pivot player 5 moves out along the lane, player 4 cuts hard around the block set by 5 and drives toward the basket expecting a pass from 3.

Chart 8

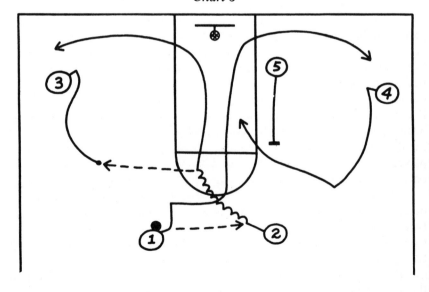

If player 3 does not make the pass, pivot player 5 may cut to the outer half of the free-throw circle and set up a blocking post or else retreat to a pivot position under the basket (side of the lane).

Player 1 will have returned to the backcourt by this time and the continuity may be continued with player 3 passing to teammate 1 and cutting for the basket.

When concentrating on an offense which features extensive use of a big man it is necessary to give consideration to the use of the control game. It is important that the big fellow have time to get to his position as well as have time to maneuver for his favorite or assigned spot in the formation.

It is also important to keep in mind that coaches who are not fortunate in having a big man or men will resort to some type of pressure defense to prevent your big man from gaining his set position in your offense. So, it is advisable that considerable attention be paid to the big man's part in meeting a pressure defense. Naturally, the big man's teammates will be charged with the responsibility of advancing the ball against the various pressure defenses (man-to-man or zone types), but the big fellow must help out. Before proceeding with the big man offense I feel that some reference should be made to the transition from high school and college basketball to professional coaching.

THE BIG MAN IN PROFESSIONAL BASKETBALL

Having played professional basketball I was not entirely unprepared for the job when I took over as head coach of the Philadelphia Warriors in the National Basketball Association. At the start, I would like to stress that coaching professional basketball may be compared with managing a major league baseball team. In professional basketball the coach operates more in the role of a manager than that of a coach. Practically all of the players are hand-picked collegiate players who have been coached through high school and college by experienced and capable mentors. From the seven or eight hundred college basketball players who are elegible for the professional basketball draft each year only a very, very few have all the attributes to "make the grade."

This means that those who are drafted are, in the great majority of cases, well drilled in the basic game fundamentals and in various types of team play. Furthermore, the players are older, more set in their ways, and therefore not susceptible to sudden changes in their use of the game skills. As stated previously, practically all professional teams use the Two-Three offense, and since man-to-man defense is required, there is nothing startling to be added from a coaching point of view.

This brings the coach head on into the personnel problem. He has a hand-picked group of players, and from this group he must develop a team which possesses the skills and the bodies to face up to a schedule which may well consist of over 120 games (schedule, exhibition, and play-off) in a period of six months. This requires that players not only be masters of the skills of the game but that they possess physical stamina which will stand up to a strenuous and lengthy schedule.

There is still another factor. This is the quality which may well be termed mental toughness. Professional basketball is a dog-eat-dog kind of game. No quarter is asked and none is given by the players making up the league. Until they arrived on the professional scene, basketball was just a sport to most of the draftees. Then, suddenly, all the glory goes out the window, and they find they have to prove themselves all over again. Basketball now becomes a business, a way of life, the means of making a living.

This is where the mental toughness comes in. The bumps are hard and the ability to come back against a poor personal showing or a bitter team defeat goes hand and hand with the drive and fighting spirit of each player, winner or loser. The professional coach looks for this mental toughness in his players and frequently gives this quality preference over expertness in game skills.

With the above factors and qualities as a start, the professional coach still must select a team. This is a most difficult problem, yet all coaches know they rise or fall on their ability to make the right selection. In professional basketball all players want to play and feel that they belong; they dread sitting the bench and often request that they be traded so they may have a chance to play instead of sitting. The coach must keep these important support players happy by using them as much as possible. Here, of course, is the rub, because the key players are anxious to add to their scoring, assists and rebounding records and demand regular action.

When I took over the Warriors I was happy to find the great Wilt Chamberlain on hand. Chamberlain, in addition to holding practically all of the NBA records, is very intelligent and coachable; he is a student of the game and wants to win.

With Chamberlain in the big man spot, the next team selections were for the corner spots. Here, one of the players was a great scorer and an outstanding team man, Paul Arizin. Mescherry, a newcomer, was a strong, agile player with the physical makeup to go with the job, and he showed signs of greatness from the first day he reported. In the backcourt I had three great players: Tom Gola topped the list, but Guy Rodgers and Attles were not far behind. All three could shoot, feed the big man, dribble, and take charge of the offense. With these six key men, the Warriors and I were on our way.

The Philadelphia Warriors Bench: Frank McGuire, Wilt Chamberlain, Tom Gola, Paul Arizin, and Al Attles.

The Boston Celtics, then as now, dominated the league. Still, we battled them right down to the wire and might have taken it all in the final game of the seven-game series but for a single point; except for a little break or two, we might have won the game and gone on from there as champions. The next year the franchise was transferred to the west coast. This change would have taken me too far away from my home and family and friends, so I sat out the second year of my contract and then took over the reins at the University of South Carolina.

In my opinion professional basketball is in its infancy. Expansion of the league is a certainty, and with the building of new and greater stadiums throughout the country the game will reach new and greater heights.

BIG MAN OFFENSE

In today's basketball it is necessary to concentrate on the big man (6 ft., 8 in. to 6 ft., 10 in.). Until rules are developed which will restrict the importance of the big man, all coaches will continue to seek out and develop more and even taller players. I have concentrated on the big man offense for many years. At St. John's University the tall player was Zawoluk; at North Carolina it was Lenny Rosenbluth; with the Philadelphia Warriors it was Wilt Chamberlain; and at South Carolina, Jim Fox. The use of the big man at South Carolina is shown in the pages which follow.

POSITIONS

The big man assumes positions 1, 2, 3 and 4 in the various formations we use (Chart 9). Naturally, our plays change when his position changes. This type of single pivot offense is used against the man-to-man defense.

By changing the position of the big man we change our patterns of play as well as our offense continuity. This enables us to use a number of variations. The following plays work on both sides of the basket, right or left.

Chart 9

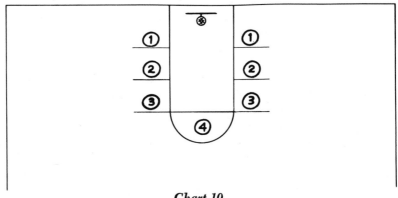

Chart 10

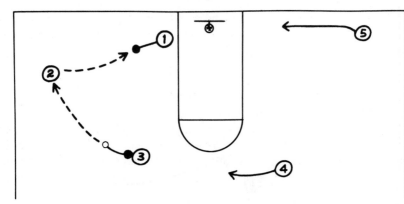

Pivot man in position 1

In this Two-Three formation player 1 must be a scorer, an expert in the execution of the shots taken in this area (Chart 10). Player 3 passes the ball to corner man 2 who is adept at feeding the pivot player. Player 5 crashes the board from the right side and player 4 remains back for defensive balance. The pivot man should have a few hand signals to show where he wants the ball to be passed.

Pivot man in position 2

The big man has moved up the lane to position 2 where he can pass off to the first or second cutter or hold the ball for a shot after his teammates have cleared past him (Chart 11). Player 4 remains back for defensive balance and player 5 may crash the boards or cut along the baseline for a pass from the big man.

Chart 11

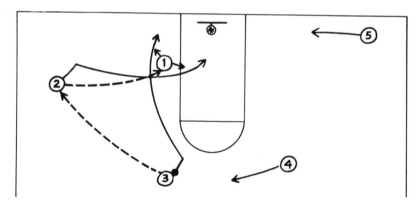

Chart 12

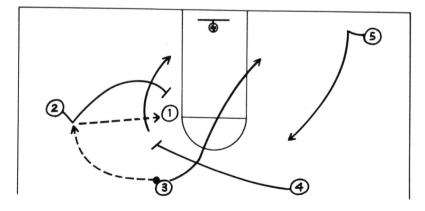

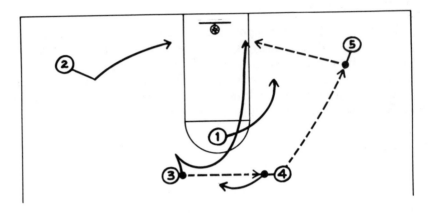

Chart 13

Pivot man in position 3

Player 3 passes the ball to 2 who feeds 1 (Chart 12). Player 2 follows his pass and sets up a double-screen with 1. Player 3 cuts through the lane to set a screen for 4. Player 5 goes back for defensive balance. (Player 4 can also go on around the double-screen for a pass from 1. A jump pass from 1 to 4 is often effective.)

Big man in position 4

Player 3 passes the ball to 4, fakes left and drives off 1 (Chart 13). Player 4 passes to 5 who forwards the ball to 3 or 1 rolling to the basket. Player 2 crashes the board and 4 remains back for defensive balance.

THE DOUBLE PIVOT

If coaches are fortunate enough to have two good big men, they use them as a double-pivot offense. This offense was used years ago at St. John's and was successful, although the pivot men were not as big as modern players.

In the double-pivot offense two big men are stationed on the sides of the lane. When outside shots are taken, the double pivot provides height inside for offensive tip-ins or possession rebounding.

Double-pivot in position 1

Player 4 passes to 5 as 1 screens for 2 (Chart 14). Player 2 receives the ball for a turn or hook shot. Player 3 fakes to the middle and goes in for the rebound. Player 4 remains back for safety.

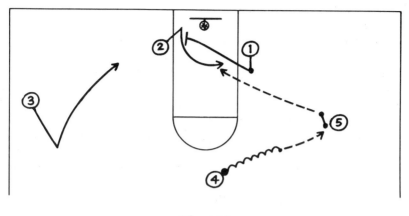

Chart 14

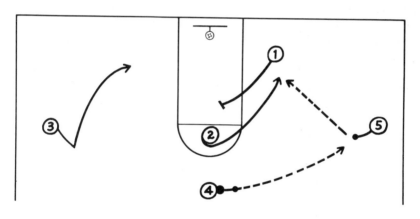

Chart 15

Pivot in position 1 and post in position 4

Player 1 screens for 2 who receives ball from 5 (Chart 15). Player 2 may shoot or pass back to 5 for an outside shot. Player 3 follows in. (If player 2 is covered, the continuity can be repeated by 1 and 2 screening back and forth until a pass is possible.)

THE FIVE-MAN GIVE-AND-GO WEAVE

The five-man weave keeps the under-basket area open and provides the basic circulation for all offenses used at South Carolina University. As a straight game offense it permits excellent use of change-of-direction tactics; inside, outside, and back screens; dribble blocks; and slicing plays.

By the use of the dribble the weave can be slowed down to permit time for all kinds of screens and blocks. Since all offensive players are constantly on the move, man-to-man opponents do not dare to sag or float. Further, the weave provides offensive and defensive court balance because of the ease with which the weave "spots" (three in the backcourt and one in each corner) are filled.

The charts here are diagrammed to the right only; naturally, all circulations and all plays may be used to the left. The diagrams are designed chiefly to illustrate the circulation and a few natural plays. The players themselves will develop many extemporaneous plays once they become aware of the possibilities.

In Chart 16 player 1 passes the ball to teammate 2 and uses a back screen to receive a return pass. Player 1 may now pass the ball to 2 (cutting with right hand raised as a target), or pass to 3 (left hand raised) who has used a slicing cut closely behind the block (three feet) set by left corner player 5. The backcourt defensive balance is set up by players 4 and 5.

In Chart 17 player 1 passes the ball to teammate 2 and sets up a block (three feet) behind 2's opponent. Player 2 passes the ball to the corner player 4. This establishes reverse circulation, since the regular circulation calls for a path toward the left and a pass to teammate 3. After passing to player 4, player 2 sets a slow-moving screen for teammate 3. Player 3 fakes left and cuts down the lane. Note again that the reverse circulation is established because player 2 changes the continuity by passing to 4 instead of 3. Players 1 and 5 are responsible for the defensive balance.

Chart 16

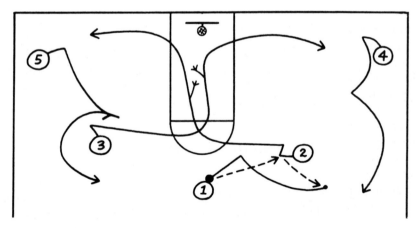

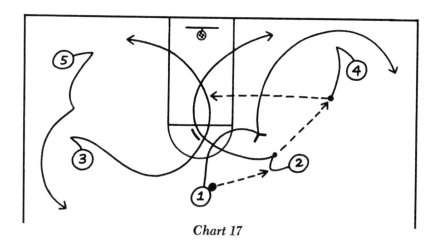

Chart 17

THE FIVE-MAN ROLL

The five-man roll usually employs the inside screen in rolling from corner to corner. The players move from the center of the court to one corner, then back to the center, and thence to the other corner in a continuous roll. The use of the inside screen protects the ball; about all the passer has to worry about is that he does not charge a teammate's guard when he executes the inside screen.

The five-man roll is used by many teams to freeze the ball. The continuous roll from corner to corner annoys many opposing teams who get impatient when the ball is held up. This attack is designed to take immediate advantage of interception attempts. Outside screens may be employed, but there is considerable risk of charging infractions. The use of the dribble is important in slowing down the roll.

In Chart 18 player 1 passes to teammate 2 and executes an inside screen as he rolls toward the right corner. Player 2 dribbles left a short distance, passes the ball to teammate 3, and executes an inside screen as he rolls to the left corner. Player 4 comes up the sideline a short distance and then moves toward the center of the court prepared to receive a pass from player 3. Player 5 also advances up the left sideline and rolls toward the center of the court expecting a pass from teammate 4. All players use the inside screen in this roll (cutting between a teammate and his opponent).

Chart 19 shows the use of outside screens in the roll. This is a difficult maneuver; to avoid contact, all players must be able to employ a pivot spin. The pivot spin when moving to the right is executed by pivoting *away* from a teammate's opponent on the *left* foot. When moving to the left, the pivot spin is made by pivoting *away* from the approaching opponent on the *right* foot.

In Chart 19 player 1 passes the ball to teammate 2 and attempts to

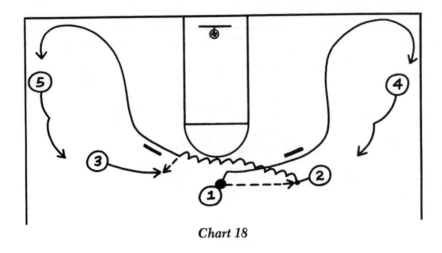

Chart 18

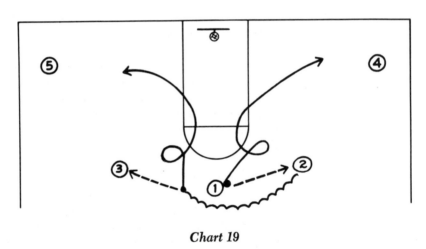

Chart 19

execute an outside screen. Because the opponent guarding teammate 2 is approaching, player 1 avoids contact by using a pivot spin from his extended *left* foot. Player 2 dribbles a short distance and then passes to teammate 3. Since the opponent guarding teammate 3 is approaching, player 2 must also pivot-spin away and back on his *right* foot to avoid contact. (The term *contact* means to charge an opponent which, naturally, is a foul.)

THE FOUR-MAN ROLL WITH A POST-PIVOT

This is a slow, possession type of offense. The use of the dribble is imperative since it is difficult for the four players taking part in the roll to cover the corner-to-corner distance. The post-pivot player is used chiefly as a block around which one of the "rollers" may dribble or cut for a pass. When one of the players is hard pressed and a teammate is covered, the post-pivot player is expected to break to the ball for safety. However, some teams employ the post-pivot player as a scoring medium from a high post position or on the side of the lane. He usually moves with the ball, trying to keep between the ball and the basket.

The rollers (players) must dribble with their outside hands, keeping their bodies between the opponents and the ball (right-hand dribble when moving to the right, left-hand dribble when moving to the left). The coach should make sure that the shoulder opposite the dribbling hand is lowered so the the dribbler may drive hard for the basket at any time and yet give the ball maximum protection.

In Chart 20 player 1 passes to teammate 2 and executes an inside screen as he rolls toward the left corner. Player 2 dribbles to the right, passes to teammate 3, and employs an inside screen on his way to the right corner. Player 3 dribbles toward the center of the court, passes to teammate 4, executes an inside screen, and moves toward the left corner. Player 4 dribbles to the right prepared to pass the ball to teammate 2, who is now rolling out from the right corner.

In Chart 21 player 1 passes to teammate 2, executes an inside screen, and continues on to the right corner. Player 2 dribbles to the left, passes the ball, and executes another inside screen. Player 3 dribbles around the screen toward the basket. Players 4 and 5 are responsible for continuing the roll to the center of the court.

In Chart 22 player 1 passes to teammate 2, executes an inside screen, and continues to the right corner to replace teammate 4. Player 2 reverses and, instead of passing the ball to teammate 3, passes to player 4. He then cuts left and establishes a block beside the lane. This sets reverse circulation in motion; player 3 immediately reverses his circula-

Chart 20

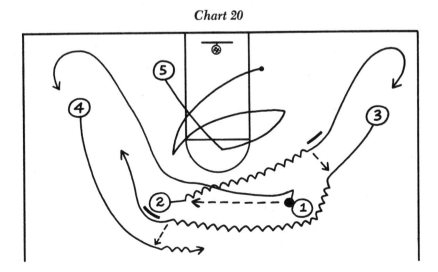

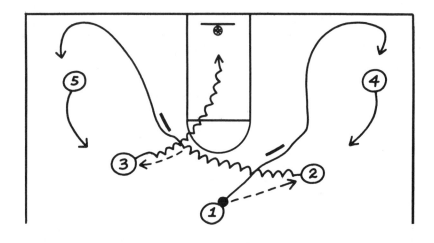

Chart 21

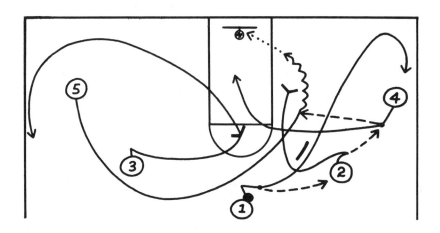

Chart 22

tion path and sets up a block in the outer half of the free-throw circle. Player 5 has rolled up the left sideline and now drives hard to the right of the two blocks and down the right side of the free-throw lane. Player 4 passes the ball to him and follows in. Players 2 and 3 reverse to the backcourt and are responsible for defensive balance.

In Chart 23 player 1 passes to teammate 2. Just before the pass is made, post player 5 drives to a post position in the outer half of the free-throw circle to a spot behind player 1 who held the ball. Now, as the ball

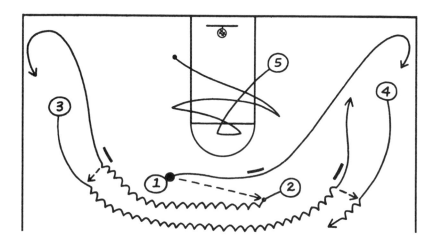

Chart 23

is passed to player 2, post-player 5 moves to a position between player 2 and the basket. Player 2 dribbles to the left, passes to teammate 3, executes an inside screen, and continues on to the left corner. Post player 5 moves with the ball as shown. Player 3 dribbles right and passes to teammate 4. During this dribbling and passing each player is watching for his or a teammate's opponent to make a mistake so a drive for the basket can be attempted.

3

basic offenses versus man-to-man defense

THE TWO-THREE OFFENSE

Position responsibilities in the Two-Three offense are as follows: The players in the back line are known as backcourt players and are expected to be fine passers, excellent outside shooters, expert dribblers, fast-break specialists, and attack organizers (quarterbacks). Two of the front-line players are called corner men and are stationed in the left and right corners. The third man is known as the post or pivot player and works along either side of the free-throw lane and/or in the outer half of the free-throw circle.

The corner players should, preferably, be tall and fast and capable of working at the post or pivot position. They should be good shots from the corners and sides of the court, masters of the jump shot, expert at driving along the baseline or out toward the outer half of the free-throw circle, possess strong follow-in ability, and be good rebounders.

The pivot or post man should be a good passer, master of the various pivot shots, a good defensive player and an expert rebounder.

One of the best methods of selecting players or determining the most outstanding is to play one against one. And, in the basic offense (Two-Three), the value of one-on-one play is not overlooked. Thousands of clutch games are won each year because a particular player on one team is superior to his opponent in one-on-one play and the team is smart enough to find it out and take advantage of the opportunity.

Naturally, the use of the one-on-one requires freedom and room to work. This means that the pivot or post player must be able to work from a corner or, if necessary, from the backcourt. This will help to keep the center of the court open and will provide the one-on-one player with enough room in which to maneuver.

Our use of the Two-Three offense is designed to give the players a certain amount of freedom yet force them to merge into a cohesive unit through a method of circulation that maintains floor balance.

The backcourt players are responsible for court balance and are expected to initiate and set up the plays. They are regarded as quarterbacks, although this responsibility will usually be taken over by the most aggressive and dominant "sparkplug." The two backcourt players employ inside, outside, and back screens, give-and-go tactics, and dribble screens and blocks. They are responsible for the movement of the ball and for offensive as well as defensive balance.

In moving and handling the ball, the backcourt players are joined and supported by the corner men. The corner men are expected to come out to the backcourt to supply defensive and court balance when a backcourt teammate cuts for the basket. This is one of the vital reasons for including them in the four-man weave.

Big men are effective in setting up post-screens. When a smaller teammate cuts around them, a switch may develop. If so, it will pit the smaller backcourt player against a taller opponent who may not be able to match the cutter's speed. The corner men are expected to supplement the post-pivot player in offensive rebounding.

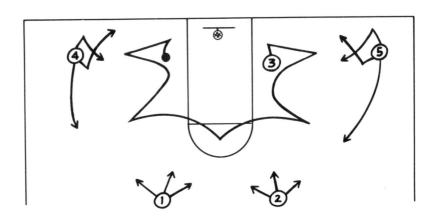

Chart 24

Development of a tall, strong player for post-pivot duties is important. This player is the key man in the Two-Three. He should have good footwork, be able to rebound, block, and handle the ball. Unless he has obtained a good scoring spot near the basket and a teammate in possession of the ball is in a favorable feeding position, he should meet all passes, using his legs and body to block his opponent away from the ball. The pivot-post man should be able to blend in with the give-and-go weave and should be an expert at one-on-one play.

Position allocations are shown in Chart 24. Players 1 and 2 are back-line (backcourt) players. Player 4 and player 5 are front-line (corner) men, and player 3 is the third front-line (pivot-post) man.

Chart 25 illustrates the usual give-and-go with player 3 setting up a turnaround play for player 2. Player 1 passes to player 2 and cuts for the basket. At the same time, the post-pivot player 3 cuts out for the ball. Player 2 gives teammate 3 a high, lob pass and cuts around the turnaround block. Player 3 (facing the basket with the ball held high over his head) will pass, shoot, or dribble in for the lay-up, depending upon the action of his opponent. Players 4 and 5 set up the defensive balance in the backcourt.

In Chart 26 player 1 passes the ball to teammate 2 and uses an inside screen to cut behind 2. Player 2 returns the ball to 1 and tries to maneuver his opponent into 1's guard and drive for the basket. Note that post-pivot player 3 is keeping his opponent busy by whirling toward the baseline. The corner men (4 and 5) come up the sidelines and will set up the defensive balance in the backcourt.

In Chart 27 player 1 passes to teammate 2 and uses an outside

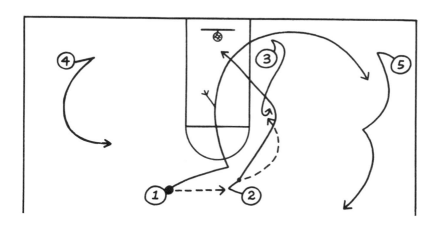

Chart 25

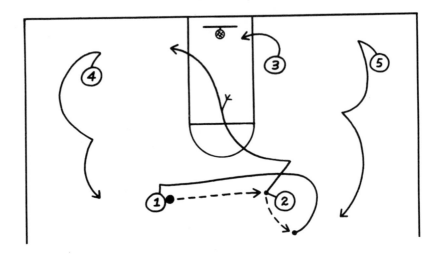

Chart 26

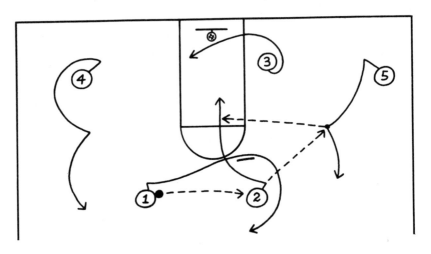

Chart 27

screen to get behind 2. Player 2 immediately passes the ball to teammate 5 and cuts for the basket. Player 3 again whirls to take his opponent out of the play and to get into position for a pass from the cutter should his opponent switch to cover player 2. Player 5 passes the ball to 2 and continues up the sideline. In this situation player 5 will follow in should a shot be taken, and players 1 and 4 will be responsible for defensive balance.

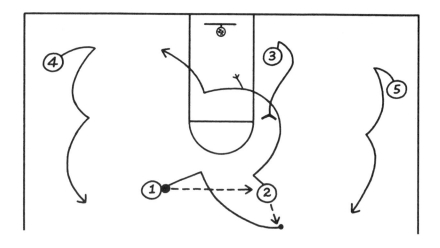

Chart 28

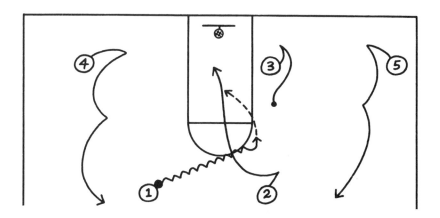

Chart 29

In Chart 28 player 1 passes to teammate 2 and uses a back screen to receive the return pass. Immediately after passing, player 2 fakes left and cuts around the block set by post-pivot player 3. Player 5 will follow in if player 1 returns the pass to the cutter 2. In this case players 1 and 4 will be responsible for the defensive balance in the backcourt.

In Chart 29 player 1 sets up a dribble-block behind teammate 2's opponent. (Note that player 1 is facing the basket.) Player 2 cuts around the block and will receive a bounce pass if he succeeds in getting free. If player 1's opponent switches, 1 may shoot or pass to post-pivot player

3. In this chart player 1 passes to teammate 2. Players 4 and 5 are responsible for defensive balance.

In Chart 30 player 1 passes to teammate 2 and cuts for the basket. Player 2 passes to post-pivot player 3 who dribbles up behind teammate 2's opponent. Player 2 holds his position until player 3 has dribbled to the block position and then uses a change-of-direction and a hard cut for the basket to get free for a return pass. Players 4 and 5 set up the backcourt defensive balance.

In Chart 31 player 1 fakes to teammate 2, then reverses and dribbles to his left. (This sets up reverse circulation.) Player 1 then passes to teammate 4, fakes right and cuts behind 4 for a return pass. Post-pivot player 3 fakes and then cuts as shown to the opposite side of the lane. Player 4 gives player 1 an over-the-shoulder pass to set him up for a set-shot clearout and then breaks for the basket. Player 1 may now shoot or may pass either to the big man or to the corner man (player 5) who has cut across court toward the ball. Player 2, on the opposite side of the court, uses the reverse circulation path and returns to the backcourt where he is joined by teammate 1 for defensive balance.

In Chart 32 player 1 fakes a pass to teammate 2 and then feeds the ball to the big man who has cut to a post position beside the free-throw line. Player 1 then fakes to the right and sets a slow, outside screen for player 4. Player 1 reverses and returns to the backcourt for defensive balance. The corner man 4 utilizes the screen by teammate 1 and cuts past teammate 3 for a hand-off. Player 2 exchanges positions with player 5 and, if a play occurs, may cut back toward the basket or rejoin teammates 1 and 5 in the backcourt.

In Chart 33 player 1 passes to teammate 2 and cuts for the basket. Player 2 fakes a return pass to player 1 and then dribbles left across court behind the moving, outside screen set by player 1. Player 3 also sets a block on the side of the lane. If player 2 is unable to continue on

Chart 30

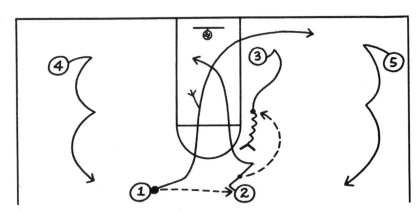

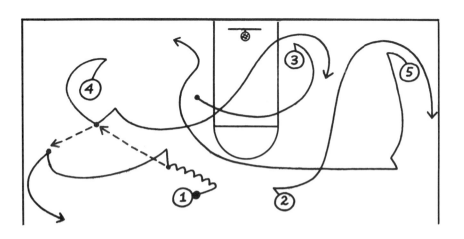

Chart 31

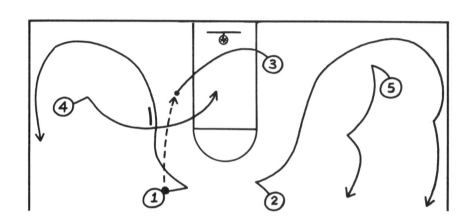

Chart 32

Chart 33

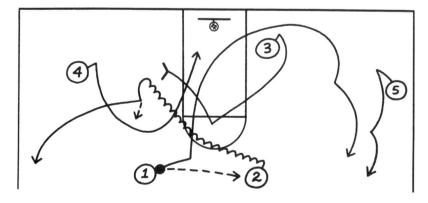

to the basket for a score, he executes a reverse pivot and attempts to feed the ball to the corner man 4 who cuts across for the hand-off. Players 1 and 2 will return to the backcourt for defensive balance.

In Chart 34 player 1 fakes to teammate 2 and then passes to the corner man 4. This sets up the reverse circulation path and 1 returns to the backcourt. Player 4 meets the pass and feeds the opposite corner man 5 who has cut around the block set by the post-pivot player 3. Player 4 follows his pass. As soon as teammate 5 clears his block, the post-pivot player 3 drops back to the outer half of the free-throw circle. Player 5 may attempt a shot if he is loose, return the ball to teammate 4, or pass to the post-pivot player 3 on the free-throw line. (Player 3 is usually free for a shot on this play.)

Chart 34

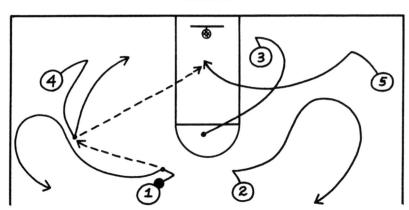

Chart 35

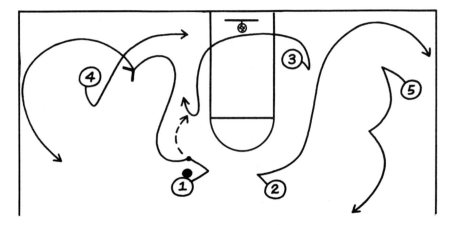

In Chart 35 player 1 fakes to teammate 2 and then reverses the circulation by lobbing a high, short pass to post-pivot player 3. Player 3 sets up the turnaround play for teammate 1 who cuts around for a possible return pass. If there is a switch, the big man 3 can shoot or dribble in for a lay-up. If he is checked and player 1 is covered, he may pass to corner man 4 who has cut around a block set by player 1. The backcourt balance is set up by players 1 and 5.

In Chart 36 player 1 dribbles to an outside-screen position behind teammate 2's opponent. He then hands-off to player 2 and continues toward the basket. Veering off to the right, he sets a block for corner player 5. Player 2 dribbles a short distance and then passes to the corner man 4. Player 2 cuts around teammate 4 expecting a return pass. If it

Chart 36

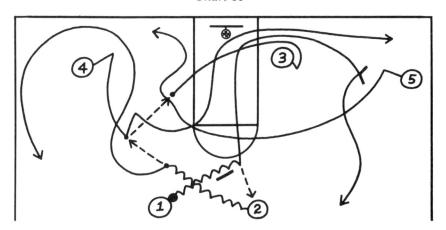

Chart 37

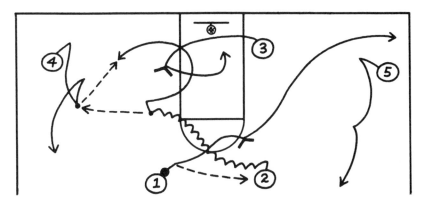

does not materialize, he cuts for the left corner and back up the sideline for defensive balance. If player 4 cannot return the ball to player 2, he feeds teammate 3 the ball and cuts for the basket. The opposite corner man 5 cuts across the lane to "split the post." If he fails to get a hand-off, he continues to the corner to replace teammate 4. Players 1 and 2 are responsible for defensive balance.

In Chart 37 player 1 passes to teammate 2 and sets a block behind 2's opponent. Player 2 fakes right and dribbles hard behind the block. If he succeeds in maneuvering his opponent into the block, he continues his dribble toward the basket. If he cannot get free, he passes to the corner man 4, executes a hard stop, and cuts behind the block set by the post-pivot player 3. Player 4 returns the pass and player 2 should be free for a scoring attempt. Players 4 and 5 are responsible for defensive balance.

In Chart 38 player 1 passes to teammate 2 and cuts for the basket. If player 2 cannot return the pass, he dribbles as shown and uses a reverse turn to set up a block for the corner man 4. The post-pivot player 3 moves across the lane to set up a double block with teammate 2. Player 4 fakes to the left, cuts across in front of the double block, and receives a hand-off from player 2. The backcourt balance is the responsibility of players 2 and 5.

In Chart 39 player 1 passes to teammate 2 and cuts for the basket. When player 2 pivots away and passes to the corner man 5, player 1 reverses his circulation path and fills the left corner spot. Player 2 fakes a return pass to cutter 1 and passes to the right corner man 5. He then cuts in front of the block set by the post-pivot player 3. If he does not get the ball, player 2 continues on around the corner and back up the sideline to the backcourt. Player 5 dribbles behind teammate 2's screen and in front of the block set by player 3. Player 1 buttonhooks around in case his opponent floats; he is prepared for the pass and a shot if

Chart 38

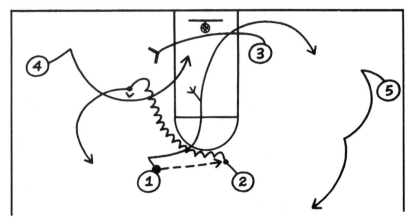

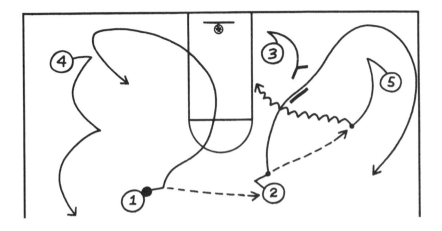

Chart 39

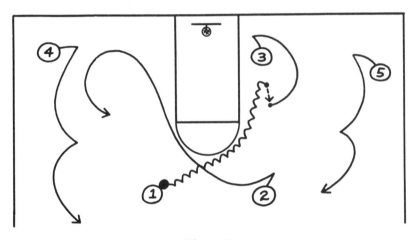

Chart 40

player 5 does not have a play. Players 2 and 4 are responsible for defensive balance.

In Chart 40 player 1 fakes a pass to teammate 2, dribbles hard to the side of the free-throw line, and sets up a pivot-block beside post-pivot player 3. Player 2 replaces teammate 4 and is prepared to cut back to the basket. The big man whirls around teammate 1 (reverse offensive play) and takes the pass for a jump shot. Players 4 and 5 are responsible for the backcourt defensive balance.

In Chart 41 player 1 initiates a give-and-go and reverses direction. At the same time, he provides a screen for pivot man 3. Player 2 passes to corner man 5, follows his pass and reaches a point behind 5. Player 5

Chart 41

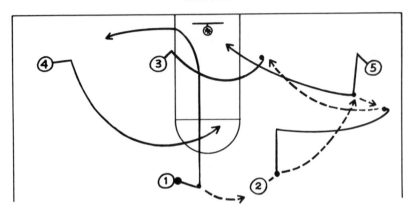

Side clear-out. (Used to get the ball to the big man in the pivot position.) The blackboard drawing illustrates the movement of the ball and players in executing a side clear-out. The ball goes from backcourt player 1 to teammate 2. Player 2 passes the ball to wing-man teammate 5 and follows his pass as shown. Wing player 5 returns the ball to teammate 2 and cuts in front of pivot player 5. There are several variations to this clear-out. Player 5 may break toward the ball from the opposite side of the lane. He (5) may reverse from the right side to provide a block for teammate 4 to cut around and to the ball under the basket. Practically all of the variations guarantee the safety of the pass against man-to-man defense.

The side clear-out in action. Player 32 passes the ball to wing player 15, follows his pass, and receives a return over-the-shoulder pass from 15. Player 15 cuts toward and around the pivot player (54), and teammate 32 has a clear pass to the big man (54) under the basket.

returns the ball to 2 with an over-the-shoulder or bounce pass and cuts as the pivot man 3 breaks behind the screen set by 1. The ball is passed by 5 to 3 in his pivot-shot position under the basket. Player 3 may shoot, pass to 5, back to 2 or to 4 breaking to the free-throw line.

In Chart 42 player 1 passes to 2 and fakes a cut. Player 2 passes to 5 and, to set a delayed timing opportunity, screens in front of 5. Player 5 returns the ball to 2 and cuts. Pivot player 3 has set a screen for corner player 4 who cuts to the ball and receives the pass. He may shoot, pass to 3 on the free-throw line or to 5 on the weak side of the court. Player 1 sets up the defensive balance.

Chart 42

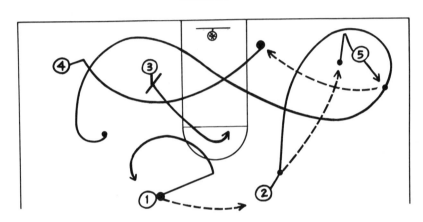

THE ONE-TWO-TWO OFFENSE

The One-Two-Two formation sets four men along the sides of the free-throw lane as shown in Chart 43. The ball is controlled by the back-court quarterback (1) who is stationed two strides in back of the head of the lane. The front and back lane players cut from side to side for screens and plays. The under-basket players (4 and 5) may set picks for their backcourt teammates (2 and 3) or cut around them and toward the ball for variations.

In Chart 44 under-basket players (4 and 5) are shown cutting toward the ball to set up post positions. Player 2 and 3 may cut to the basket and continue to the sides to take up wing positions for variation plays. The accompanying photographs illustrate a few of the basic plays which are possible. Many variations of this style of play permit blending into the basic offense—Two-Three.

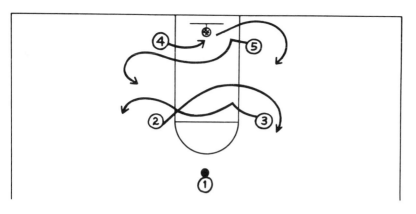

Chart 43

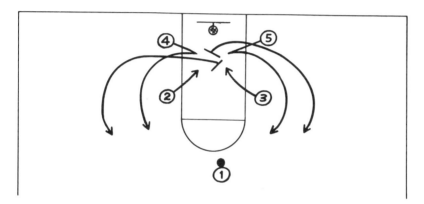

Chart 44

This blackboard drawing shows the first of the two basic moves in the One-Two-Two "Box" offense. The wing man and the under-basket big man are executing a simple lateral cross which leads to an entire repertory of plays.

The lateral cross in action. Offensive backcourt player 44 has the ball, and the wing players 31 and 32 are crossing as are the under-basket players 20 and 13. The play here is designed to free wing player 21 for a shot. Wing player 31 screens 21's defensive opponent (32) away from teammate 21 who receives the ball from 44 and, after faking a drive, manages to get off a one-hand set shot which sinks for two points.

The second of the two basic moves in the One-Two-Two "Box" offense is shown in this blackboard drawing. The under-basket big men (players 4 and 5) are using their wing teammates (players 2 and 3) as blocking posts in breaking out to the ball. The break-out may be made by one or both big men, according to the play.

Basic move number two of the One-Two-Two offense in skeleton form. Players 13 and 31 are using teammates 24 and 23 as blocking posts in their moves to "meet" the press. Backcourt player 44 selects teammate 13 for the pass, and 13 gets the shot away. Note the post players (23 and 24) are following-in the shot.

Basic move number two in action. Here, players 13 and 31 again have used 23 and 24 as posts to cut around and toward the ball, which 13 has received from backcourt quarterback 44. Player 13 gets set and makes a jump shot.

One-Two-Two offense wing variation in action. Wing players 15 and 32 have broken out to sideline (wing) positions. When the ball is passed to teammate 15, player 32 (not seen in picture) cuts toward the left corner. The backcourt quarterback (22) passes the ball to teammate 15 on the right side of the court (wing position). Simultaneously, players 20 and 45 initiate a lateral move, and 15 passes the ball to 20 who has cut around teammate 45's screen. Defensive player 24 makes the mistake of going "behind" in trying to follow his opponent (20), and the pass from 15 to 20 is uncontested. Player 20 has ample time for a shot but notices that the headhunter (defensive player 21) is out of position and has turned his head. Player 45 sees the opening and cuts for the basket. Player 20 passes the ball to the cutter (45) for an easy lay-up score.

4

the basic
zone offenses

Zone defenses vary so much in formation and usage that it is impossible to teach a specific attack to meet all the types that may be encountered in a particular season. It is far better to teach one or two basic offenses and depend upon these to meet the various zones, changing their alignment as changes are found necessary to meet the peculiarities of the various zones encountered.

At South Carolina University we use the One-Three-One and the Two-Two-One formations as our basic zone offenses. We have found that we can meet any type of zone with these two formations. We try to use these two basic zone-offense formations in such manner that we outnumber one defensive part of the zone. Then we center our attack at this point.

In attacking any zone we try, naturally, to use the fast break to reach attacking territory before the opponents can get their defensive zone set up. When we are unable to develop a fast-break situation, we slow down and adapt one of our two basic offenses to the type of zone our opponents employ.

Scouting notes usually suffice to acquaint us with the type of zone and any variations being used. It is at this point that our "quarterback" becomes important, since we must assume that our opponents may plan special defensive measures for us. He must assume the responsibility of setting up the One-Three-One or the Two-Two-One attacking formation. However, all of our players have been familiarized with their assigned positions and duties and advance to them confidently with little lost time. As soon as the opponents' type of zone is revealed, the players recognize the plays necessary and attack immediately.

We emphasize the short pass; player movement from the rear (behind the zone opponents); a strong follow-in game; shots down the middle (from the backcourt right on through the free-throw-circle area and into the lane); shots from the sides and corners; and player replacement (when a player cuts, he usually pulls an opponent away from that particular zone area).

Our players are aware that a zone loses much of its strength when they can make it move and keep it moving. Further, they realize that a zone that can be opened up (spread) leaves openings from which good shots may be obtained. Constant movement with the use of short, fast passes and the elimination of bad shots means success.

Dribbling, bouncing the ball, holding up the passing, too much use of feints and fakes, cross-court passes, and bunching the offense work to the advantage of the zone. So the rule is to keep the ball hopping and to use the planned and practiced moves necessary to force openings for good shots.

There are a great number of zone formations, but we have found that our competitors show preference for the various types in the following order:

1. Two-One-Two zone
2. Two-Three zone
3. One-Two-Two zone
4. Three-Two zone
5. One-Three-One zone

With this classification as a starting point, we utilize our two basic zone offenses to set up attacks as shown in Chart 45.

The zone alignments shown in Chart 53 (see page 86) are used only to permit the presentation of the basic zone defenses. Naturally, the movements of the attacking players and the progress of the ball result in various zone shifts. If the basic zone offenses do not work as applied to the various zone defenses, one may be substituted for the other. A few of the changes in the offensive moves and the probable zone reactions follow.

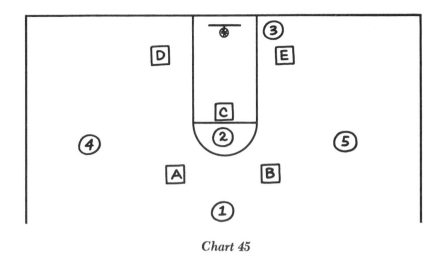

Chart 45

THE ONE-THREE-ONE ZONE OFFENSE

Position requirements

In Chart 45 player 1 is the key player and must keep moving so that he may serve as a safety point to which the ball may be returned in an emergency. Player 2 is the expert ball handler. He moves constantly, forcing his opponent C to stay with him. He must not only be a good ball handler but must have a good one-hand set and jump shot. The sideline players, 4 and 5, are expected to exchange positions and to team up with player 1 in establishing defensive balance and in protecting the ball. They also assist teammate 3 in outnumbering the defensive rebounders D and E.

Attacking the Two-Three zone defense

In Chart 46 the One-Three-One offense is used against the Two-Three zone defense. The Two-Three zone attempts to protect areas close to the basket. This leaves the middle open from sideline to sideline so that players 2, 4, and 5 should have many good scoring opportunities.

Players 1, 2, 4, and 5 keep the ball hopping and move to set up offensive triangles against all three players of the back line of the zone defense. Players 4 and 5 must be good side shots and careful passers. They do most of the cutting and share the ball-handling responsibility with teammate 2.

Player 3, on the baseline, sets up three-on-two situations against opponents D and E by working to and around the corners. He should possess a good corner shot.

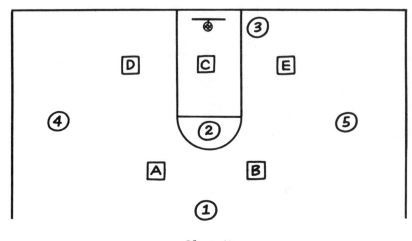

Chart 46

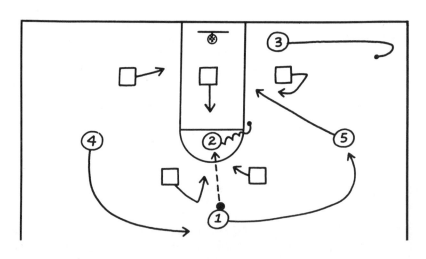

Chart 47

In Chart 47 player 1 passes directly to the post player 2 and moves to the right to replace player 5. Player 2 pivots as soon as he gets the ball and takes one bounce preparatory to taking a shot. As soon as player 2 gets the ball, teammate 5 cuts for the basket and the baseline player moves to the corner. Player 4 replaces teammate 1 in the backcourt for defensive balance. Player 2 may shoot or pass to teammate 3, 5, or 1.

Attacking the Two-One-Two zone defense

The effectiveness of the attack against the Two-One-Two zone rests largely in the hands of player 2. Rapid movement of the ball between players 1, 2, 4, and 5 puts constant pressure on defensive chasers A and B who cannot possibly cover the entire width of the court.

The baseline player 3 moves from side to side, holding the defensive rebounders D and E in place. Player 3 follows in all shots, breaks out to keep the ball moving in the under-basket attack, and fills the corners. The strength of the Two-One-Two zone lies in the under-basket defensive triangle. The weakness is on the sides and in the corners.

In Chart 48 player 1 passes to teammate 4 and replaces player 5 on the right sideline. Player 3 cuts to the left corner and receives the pass from player 4. Player 4 replaces teammate 1. Player 2 moves toward the corner, and player 5 moves at the same time. Player 3 with the ball should be able to shoot or to pass to player 2 or to player 5 who can advance along the baseline. If player 3 passes to teammate 2, he will cut toward the lane as shown. This is a counter-clockwise circulation and is effective because it attacks from behind the zone.

In Chart 49 player 1 passes to teammate 5 and follows his pass to replace player 5. Player 5 passes to teammate 2 and cuts for the right corner. Player 3 cuts away from the ball to the other side of the court. Player 4 replaces teammate 1 in the backcourt. Player 2 should be able to shoot or pass to teammate 3, 5, or 1.

Chart 48

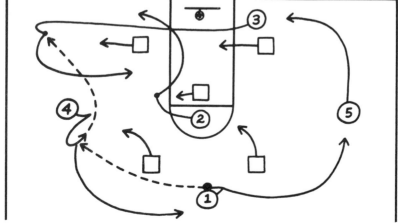

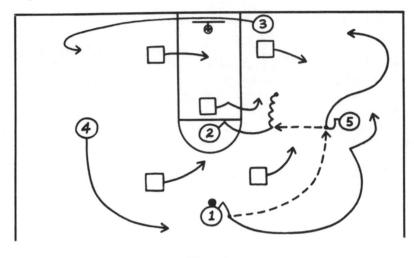

Chart 49

Attacking the One-Three-One zone defense

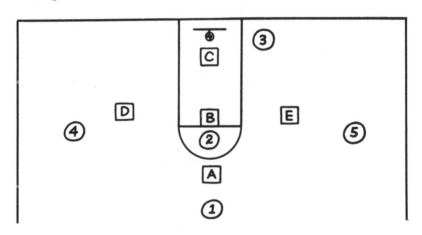

Chart 50

Chart 50 shows the One-Three-One offense used to attack the One-Three-One zone defense. This defense is weak in the corners and along the sidelines. Although it appears to be wide open under the basket, this is not necessarily true. The defense was originated by Clair Bee (former coach at Long Island University) with the express purpose of stopping the big man and has been effective in doing so. The alignment of players lends itself to excellent use of the fast break.

The One-Three-One attacking formation as shown appears to match the zone players on a man-to-man basis. However, this situation changes as soon as the ball is passed and the defensive players begin to use their moves and slides.

Player 1 is the quarterback of the attack and, with the assistance of teammates 2, 4, and 5, must get the ball into the corner and under-basket area. Then the corners are attacked by players 2, 4, and 3 on the left side and by players 2, 5, and 3 on the right side. Players 1, 4, and 5 are responsible for the defensive balance.

In Chart 51 player 1 dribbles to the right, passes the ball to team-mate 5, and reverses to the left side to replace teammate 4. Player 5 passes the ball to teammate 3 who has moved to the corner. Player 5 then replaces player 1 for backcourt defensive balance. Player 2 cuts directly down the lane and then breaks right to receive the ball from player 3. Player 4 cuts from behind the zone to the basket. Player 2 may attempt a shot or pass the ball to teammate 3 or 4. If these players are covered, he can pass the ball to teammate 1 who waits on the weak side.

In Chart 52 player 1 dribbles to the right and passes to teammate 2. Player 2 fakes a shot and passes to player 3. Player 3 pivots around prepared to shoot. Player 4 breaks from the weak side toward the basket and along the baseline. Player 5 on the right side does likewise. After his pass, player 2 cuts to the right as shown. Player 3 may shoot or pass to teammate 5, 4, or 2. Player 1 remains in the backcourt for defensive balance.

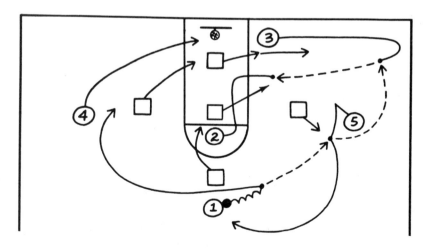

Chart 51

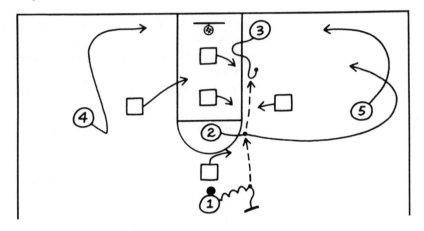

Chart 52

Two-Two-One offense

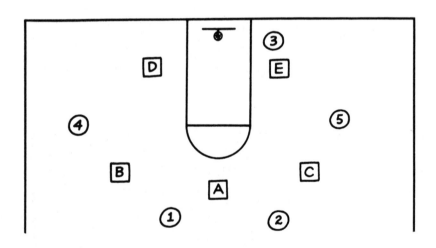

Chart 53

In Chart 53 attacking players 1, 2, 4, and 5 outnumber opponents
A, *B*, and *C* and should be able to move the ball until they secure the
opening they desire.

The presence of player 3 working along the baseline holds rebounders *D* and *E* more or less in position and leaves plenty of scoring
area near the basket. Once the ball passes the front defensive line of

A, B, and C, attacking players 4, 5, and 3 have a three-two advantage and should employ it to secure sure shots.

Players 4 and 5 are expected to assist teammates 1 and 2 in setting up defensive balance. Should 1 or 2 cut through into the front court, player 4 or player 5 must drop back to help maintain defensive balance.

Attacking the One-Two-Two zone defense

In Chart 54 the Two-Two-One offense is used to meet the One-Two-Two zone defense. This zone defense is a bunched defense and is vulnerable to medium-length shots. Since it closely resembles a Three-Two defense, it has the same fast-break strength. Players 1 and 2 should be able to handle this situation since they outnumber defensive opponent A. With the assistance of teammates 4 and 5 they always have a four-on-three advantage.

The presence of player 3 working along the baseline is a constant threat to defensive players D and E and forces them to remain in position. This provides an opportunity for sideline players 4 and 5 to work with 3 in outnumbering one of the rebounders. When opponents B and C drop back to help out one of the backcourt players, 1 or 2 can drive through for a shot or to assist in the outnumbering.

The Two-Two-One surrounds the One-Two-Two zone in Chart 55. Player 1 passes to teammate 2 and replaces him for defensive balance. Player 2 passes to teammate 5 and follows his pass to replace 5. As player 5 receives the ball, player 3 breaks to a post position on the lane. Player 5 passes the ball to teammate 3 and cuts to the corner. Player 4, on the weak side, cuts behind the zone and under the basket. Player 3 may shoot or pass to teammate 4, 5, or 2.

Chart 54

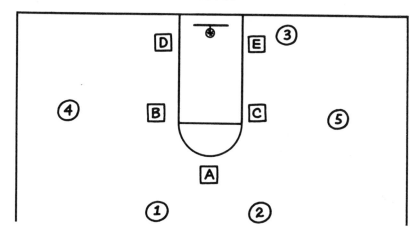

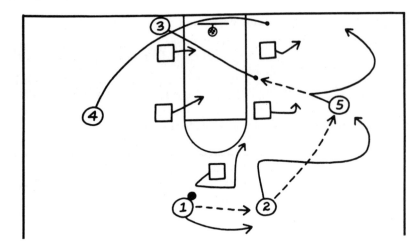

Chart 55

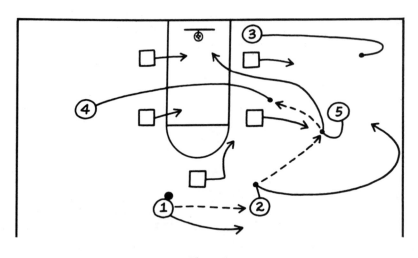

Chart 56

In Chart 56 player 1 passes to teammate 2 and replaces him for defensive balance. Player 2 passes to teammate 5 and follows his pass to replace player 5. Player 4, on the weak side, cuts across to a post position on the right side of the lane. Player 5 passes the ball to teammate 4 and drives for the basket. Player 3 moves to the right corner. Player 4 may now attempt a shot or pass to teammate 3, 5, or 2.

Attacking the Three-Two zone defense

In Chart 57 player 1 passes the ball to teammate 2 and follows the pass to replace 2. Player 2 passes to teammate 5 and follows his pass to replace 5. As soon as player 5 gets the ball, player 3 breaks out beside the lane and receives the pass from player 5. Player 4 breaks from behind the zone and along the baseline and under the basket. Player 3 may attempt a shot or pass to teammate 5, 4, or 2.

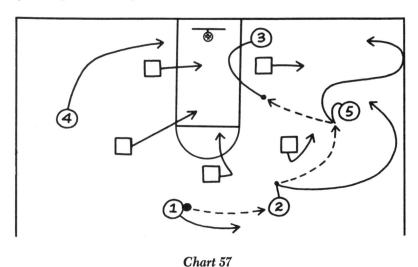

Chart 57

Attacking the Two-One-Two zone defense

Chart 58

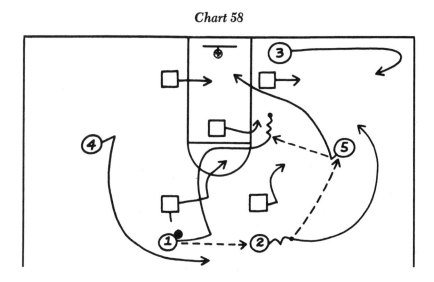

Instead of the usual One-Three-One offense against the Two-One-Two zone defense, in Chart 58 the Two-Two-One attack is used. Player 1 passes to teammate 2 and delays. Player 2 passes to teammate 5 on the right and follows his pass to replace 5. Player 1 cuts directly at the middle defensive player and then swerves to the right and receives the ball from teammate 5. Player 5 immediately cuts for the basket. Player 3 moves toward the right corner along the baseline. Player 4 replaces player 1 in the backcourt for defensive balance. Player 1 may now shoot or pass to teammate 3, 5, or 2.

The Two-Two-One attack is again used against the Two-One-Two defense in Chart 59. Player 1 passes to teammate 2 and replaces 2. Player 2 passes to teammate 5 on the right and follows his pass to replace 5. Player 5 passes to teammate 3 who has cut to the right corner, and then 5 cuts for the basket. Player 4 on the left delays until the ball is passed to teammate 3 and then cuts as shown. Player 3 now may pass to teammate 5, 4, or 2, or he may shoot from the corner.

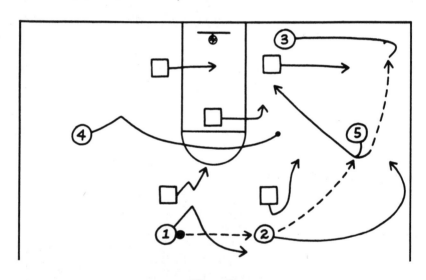

Chart 59

5

offensive game situations

The use of signals is not restricted to indicating the direction of the tap and the receiver in jump-ball situations. Certain signals or signs may be used in calling a time-out, determining a change of offense or defense, exchanging opponents in the man-to-man defense, and transferring follow-in assignments.

Many coaches are satisfied with securing possession of the ball in held-ball situations; others design certain plays from the center jump and the held-ball situations. Time-outs are precious in determining strategic moves in the closing minutes of a game, and some sort of an arrangement should be agreed upon so that the coach can control the calls. Although the rules permit any player to call for a time-out, it should not be called without the approval of the coach unless a player is injured.

Today, game strategy calls for team cohesion in changing from one offense to another. Some sort of a signal or sign should be devised for use between the coach and the captain and between the captain and teammates in deciding when one offense may be substituted for another; when a man-to-man defense may be changed to a zone; when a full- or half-court press may be applied; when players' defensive assignments are to be switched from one opponent to another because of advantages or disadvantages in size, speed, drive, or other superiority; and in transferring offensive follow-in assignments when it is obvious that a certain opponent is poorly trained in blocking out.

Signals may range from the old, familiar cloth-and-skin type to use of the eyes, called-out numbers, body facing, positions of the feet or the hands. These signals may be further complicated by being used while standing or moving, talking or silent, and by the responsibility of giving the signals changing from one player to another during the game.

The cloth-and-skin signals are indicated by the hands, touching the face, arms, legs, shirt, or trunks. For example, in the center jump or in a held-ball situation, the player giving the signals may touch his right temple to designate a tap to the left forward position. The left hand can be used similarly to designate the right forward position. Touching the chin with either hand may designate the respective guard positions, and touching the legs—right or left and with the right or left hand—may serve to designate taps directly to the side, to the front (long or short), and directly back (long or short).

The use of called numbers may serve to set up a certain offense or a play. One of the outstanding professional teams in the country signifies certain offensive plays through called numbers. Another gives signals by the player's raising a hand in the air, determining the play or formation by the number of fingers.

A change of defense or the application of some phase of the press may be signalled by the captain. Some teams give the signals after the scoring of a free throw or a goal from the field. And some coaches make the changes during a time-out. However, the change should be made if possible during play on the court to incorporate the element of surprise.

JUMP-BALL TEAM PLAY

Center-tap plays are not nearly as important as in the days of the center jump following a score. In a close game, however, the advantage to be gained in obtaining possession in more than half of the 15 or 20 times a held ball occurs during a game may mean the difference between victory and defeat. To win close games a team must at least break even in the recovery of the ball in these situations.

The chief concern in any jump-ball situation is to make sure of possession. The opening tap for each half and those at the beginning of the quarters are important because they enable a team to take control of the game, to get the feel of the ball. In the overtime period or periods, possession from the tap is vitally important because of the limited time left to play.

The development of plays from the center-tap and jump-ball situations implies control of the tap. However, the prevalence of tall players in basketball today means that practically all teams have one or more fine jumpers and there is always the chance of loss of the tap. Further, the setting up of worthwhile plays means that defensive balance must be weakened in some spot.

At South Carolina University we prefer to make sure of possession of the ball. Plays are disregarded until the ball is securely in hand. This does not mean that the center-tap and jump-ball situations are neglected. Far from it. Considerable time is devoted to jump-ball formations and all players are given positive assignments. These assignments are defined by the signals used in designating the position to which the ball will be tapped and the screening or blocking necessary by teammates to free the receiver.

The deep back tap shown in Chart 60 is an almost sure possession tap, provided that each player does his job. The objective is to get the ball at all costs. Player 1 is expected to tap the ball as far behind him as possible in the direction of his opponents' basket. Teammates 2 and 3 are in a good blocking position and must keep opponents B and C from following the ball. That is their only responsibility. Player 4 or player 5 or both are assigned to go get the ball. Good bluffing is important here since the opponents will make it tough to get the ball if they are aware of the play. Maneuvering by players 4 and 5 as if they expect to get the ball will help. As soon as player 1 strikes the ball backwards, players 4 and 5 will dash downcourt for the ball. This is a fairly safe play even if it fails, since all of the circle players, 1, 2, 3, 4, and 5, are in proper defensive positions.

Chart 61 shows a fairly safe front-court jump-ball play. Player 1 must be considered a better jumper than his opponent A. The ball is tapped slightly forward to teammate 4. Player 3 cuts around behind

Chart 60

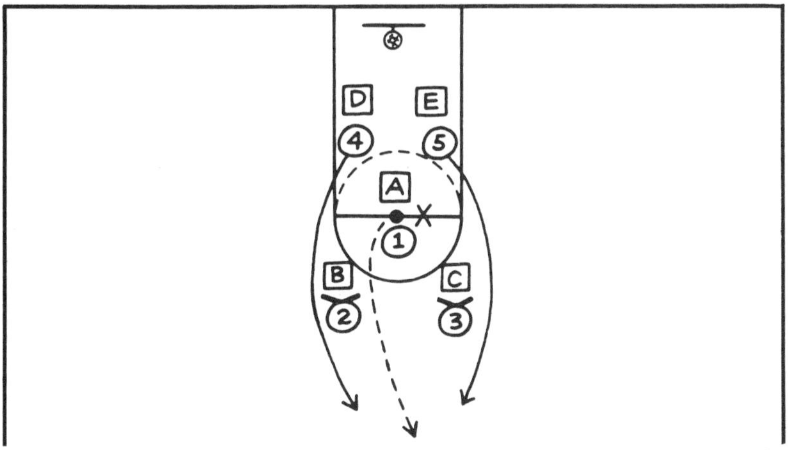

teammate 2 and will continue on toward the basket should player 4 get the ball. As soon as player 3 passes, player 2 must drop back fast for defensive balance. If the tap is lost, players 3 and 4 dash for the back-court to pick up opponents. If player 4 gets the ball he may shoot, pass to teammate 5, teammate 1 (the jumper), or to teammate 3 driving for the basket.

Chart 61

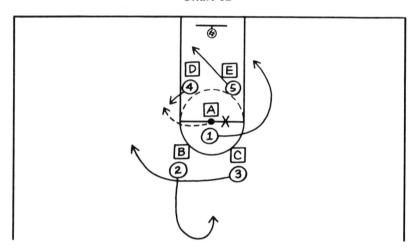

Chart 62

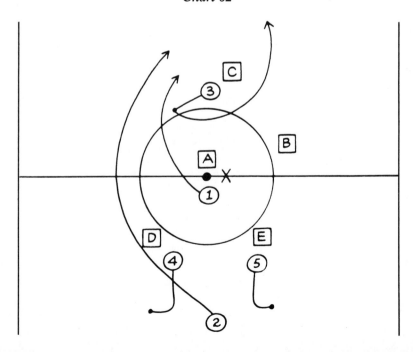

Chart 62 shows a center-jump formation that offers good protection with some opportunity to secure the ball when the jumpers are about equal in leaping ability. Naturally, opponent B may not maintain the position shown in the chart. The use of the deep back tap is evidenced by the player positions shown in the chart. If any other tap is attempted, it must be to player 3 and away from his opponent. In the illustration, player 1 taps to his left and player 3 secures the ball. Player 2 drives away from his opponent B and cuts past the screen provided by teammate 4 and 4's opponent D. The center 1 breaks in front of the post set by the tap receiver 3 and drives for the basket. Player 3 may pass to teammate 2 or to the center 1, or may dribble in for a shot. If he passes the ball to a teammate, he reverses and drives for the basket. Players 4 and 5 provide defensive balance.

A back tap by player 1 in the Chart 63 setup is dangerous. Teammates 4 and 5 are busy defending against D and E who are in good shooting positions. The ball should be always tapped to the sides or far downcourt when opponents such as B and C are playing tightly up against teammates 2 and 3. In the chart player 1 taps the ball to teammate 2 and cuts to the right of the official. Player 3 cuts diagonally as in a fast break. If teammate 2 passes the ball to 1, he will dribble down the center of the court while players 2 and 3 fill the outside lanes.

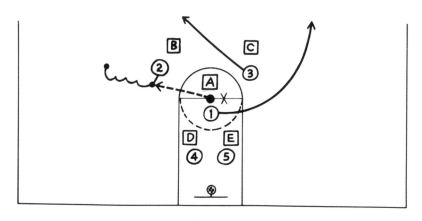

Chart 63

OUT-OF-BOUNDS PLAYS

Out-of-bounds plays occur in about the same proportion as held-ball plays. However, the scoring possibilities are far greater, particularly in under-basket plays. A quick score from an out-of-bounds play shakes the confidence of opponents and increases the scoring team's morale. Hundreds of clutch games are won each year by the use of well-executed out-of-bounds plays in the closing minutes or seconds of a close game. This is sufficient reason for the use of considerable practice time to perfect the plays.

Sideline out-of-bounds plays from the center of the court do not lend themselves as effectively to scoring possibilities as do those under the basket. However, they are more easily intercepted and are designed and practiced because the threat of a score makes the opponents guard the under-basket area and lessens interception attempts.

Out-of-bounds plays should be well planned and should be adapted to the abilities of the respective players. Each player should have a definite assignment. The best passer should handle the ball out of bounds. He will usually be one of the backcourt quarterbacks, preferably the taller of the two. Some teams press one of the front-court players, the big man or a corner man, into use when the ball goes out of bounds under the basket. A backcourt player takes the ball out of bounds in other situations.

The player who takes the ball out of bounds must keep the ball moving, faking right and left and up and down; he must avoid telegraphing his pass. Some sort of a signal should be used to initiate the movement of the players and the pass of the ball in court.

The big man should be placed near the basket if possible and used for blocking purposes or as the receiver of a high, safety pass. Spot shooters should be placed in the formation so that they can cut to the positions from which they shoot best. Each out-of-bounds play should have several options and each play should look and start alike.

In Chart 64 players 3 and 1 cut as shown and hold block positions on the right side of the lane. Player 5 holds his position until the cutter

Chart 64

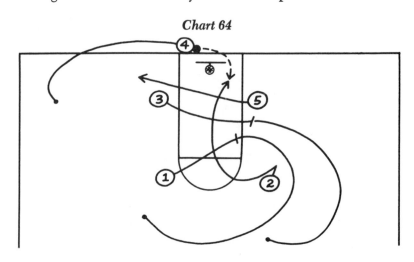

2 passes. Then 5 cuts across the lane. The play is intended for player 2. Other receivers are teammate 5 and players 1 and 2 who have cut to the backcourt to set up defensive balance.

In Chart 65 player 2 cuts first across in front of teammate 1. Player 3 cuts as before to a block position on the right side of the lane. Player 5 holds his position until the cutter 1 has cleared behind him and then cuts to the backcourt for defensive balance. Player 3 also waits until the cutter 1 clears before moving to the backcourt. Player 1 fakes right and cuts behind teammates 2, 3, and 5 for the basket.

In Chart 66, depending upon how he is played by his opponent, player 1 cuts to the right or to the left. Here he cuts left and receives the ball from player 4. Player 4 cuts in bounds. As soon as player 1 gets the ball, teammates 2, 3, and 5 move as shown. Players 2, 3, and 5 must be aware that the three-second rule is effective as soon as teammate 1

Chart 65

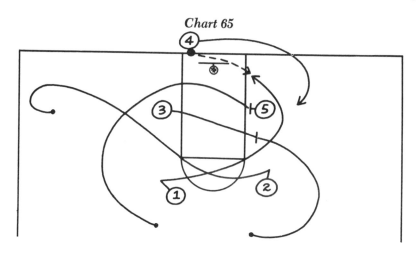

Chart 66

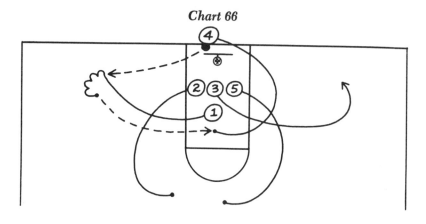

receives the ball and they must make sure to get out of the lane. After passing the ball to teammate 1, player 4 circles as shown for the return pass and a shot in front of the basket. If player 4 is unable to pass to 1, he passes to 3 who cuts to the right corner.

Chart 67 shows four players now spread across the lane. Players 2, 3, and 5 hold their positions until player 1 cuts behind them and to the right corner. Then player 2 drops straight back. Player 4 passes the ball to teammate 1 and cuts through the hole left by teammate 2. Players 3 and 5 must get out of the lane as soon as teammate 1 receives the pass to avoid the three-second penalty. If player 1 is not free for the pass, player 4 will pass to teammate 2, 3, or 5. If player 1 gets the ball, he will watch for his out-of-bounds teammate 4 and return the ball as shown if possible.

Chart 67

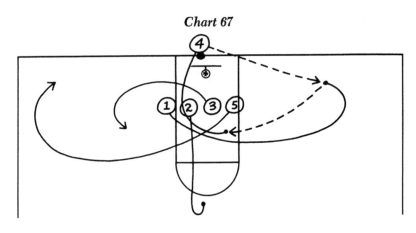

Chart 68

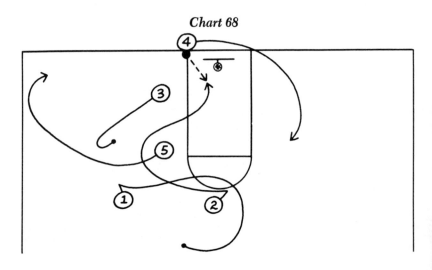

In Chart 68 player 1 cuts in front of teammate 2 and back to the backcourt for defensive balance. Player 5 holds fast until player 2 cuts behind him. Then he cuts for the left corner. Player 3 backs up as soon as the cutting signal is given by player 4 (with the ball). Player 4 may pass to teammate 2 as shown or to teammate 3, 5, or 1 in that order.

In Chart 69 player 1 screens across in front of teammate 2 and goes to the right corner. Players 3 and 5 hold fast until player 2 has cut behind them. Then they move as shown. The play is really set up

Chart 69

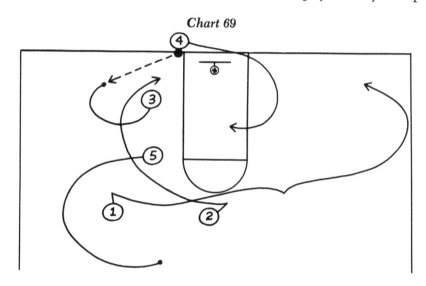

Chart 70

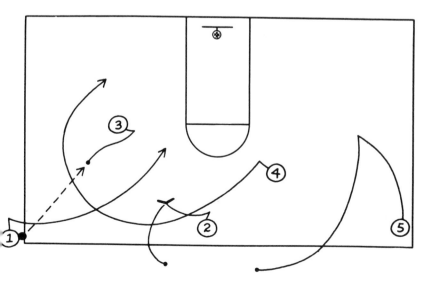

for the pivot man 3. If player 4 cannot pass to 3, he should pass to players 1 or 5. Naturally, if the cutter 2 gets free, player 4 will pass the ball to him before considering player 3.

The chief concern in Chart 70 is safe possession of the ball. Player 3 is the big man and the best ball handler. He comes in high in the air after faking toward the basket. Player 1 gives him a high pass and cuts for the basket as shown. Player 2 moves to his left and sets a block for teammate 4 who cuts around the block and joins teammate 1 in splitting the post set by player 3. Player 5 cuts hard for the basket and then reverses to the backcourt for a safety pass and defensive balance. Player 2 holds his block until teammate 4 passes and then retreats for defensive balance. If player 1 cannot hit teammate 3, he passes to player 4, 5, or 2, in that order.

PLAYING THE LANE

The position of a defensive player next to the basket on each side of the lane when a free throw is being attempted has lessened the opportunities for the offensive team to secure the ball following an unsuccessful free throw. Despite the handicap, however, many players occupying the outside offensive positions have the necessary coordination and timing ability to get a good tap-in position. If a follow-in tap shot is impossible, some of these players retain possession for their team by slapping the ball back to the shooter or to the defensive teammates in the backcourt.

Frequently, a rebound will be deep enough to reach the shooter on the free-throw line. He should be prepared to "put the ball back up" and concentrate on making the second shot. If he is too closely pressed to get the shot away, he can tap the ball back to the teammates behind him who are setting up the defensive balance.

It is important that the players of both teams make sure that they do not make contact with the lines or enter the lane until the ball has touched the backboard or the rim of the basket.

THE CONTROL GAME

Control basketball is as important as the popular run-and-fire game. And, contrary to the opinion of many people, the control game can provide just as many tense and dramatic moments as the high-geared firehouse brand of basketball. When teams play good defensive basketball, the scoring of a single basket may be as thrilling as a half dozen of the run-and-throw variety.

Control basketball implies that the ball is carefully protected and controlled through good passing and screening until an almost sure shot is possible. However, "control" applies to the mental as well as the physical aspect of the game. Team play is the essence. Individual play must be forgotten in the interest of the style of play; every player must be sold on the value of attempting good shots and, defensively, on playing hard and aggressively so that his opponent will not have a good scoring opportunity.

Control basketball is not limited to offensive play. Defensive play is equal in importance. Emphasis is placed on making as few offensive errors as possible (bad passes, forced shots, traveling, excessive dribbling, violation of the three-second rule, failure to set up defensive balance) and, through expert defensive play, forcing the opponents into making costly errors. This all means that the coach and the players must be prepared to spend as much time in the development of a strong defense as a strong offense.

Many plays are possible from the formation shown in Chart 71 but the emphasis here is placed on possession. On the signal, player 3 drops straight back one long step. Player 2 cuts as shown, and player 4

Chart 71

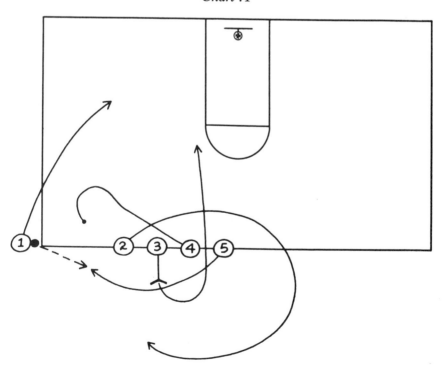

holds fast. Player 3 waits until teammate 5 has passed behind him and then cuts around teammate 4 and toward the basket. As soon as teammate 3 has passed him, player 4 cuts diagonally and hooks back. Player 1 (out of bounds) should pass to 5 if possible. If this pass is not possible he should pass to player 2, 3, or 4, in that order.

Most players regard offensive play as fun and defensive play as work. With the proper approach, however, playing good defense can give the real basketball player as much personal satisfaction as passing, screening, or shooting the ball. It is important that the coach make clear to his squad by emphasis and the allotment of time that he considers defensive play as important as offensive play. Most coaches are prone to become involved in the teaching of passing, dribbling, and shooting to the extent that they fail to spend an equal amount of time in defensive work.

There is no special system that can be termed control basketball. It is not a matter of special offensive systems or defensive styles. Control basketball will work as well with the five-man give-and-go weave as with any other style. Oklahoma A.&M. uses the four-man roll with a post-pivot. San Francisco uses a Two-Three formation. At South Carolina University we adapt the control game to our regular offensive pattern and the use of the Two-Three formation. To repeat, the success of the control game depends upon the attitude of the players. If they have been sufficiently drilled in maintaining possession of the ball until they get a good shot close to the basket, and if they will play an aggressive defensive game, the style of play will be a success. In our own case, we consider control of the ball vital in meeting teams who overmatch us in height or speed; and we have used the control method successfully in many important games.

FREEZING THE BALL

The freeze in Chart 72 is patterned after the give-and-go weave except that here the passer cuts *away* from the receiver. The players in the corners hold their positions as long as possible before advancing up the sidelines. Even then, they constantly threaten to cut for the basket. Player 1 dribbles toward the right and passes to teammate 2. Note that player 2 starts a hard cut for the basket before reversing. In this widespread formation the change-up can often be used to break free for an easy lay-up. The middle of the court and the under-basket area must be kept free. Player 2 dribbles towards the left and passes to player 3. Player 3 has cut down the left sideline before retreating to get the ball. After passing to teammate 3, player 2 cuts for the right corner to replace teammate 4. Should a teammate be double-teamed or tied up, one of the corner men breaks for the basket and up the middle for a pass.

The principle emphasized here is to spread the defense and allow the man with the ball plenty of room in which to operate. Opponents are kept busy so they will not have time to attempt to double-team the man with the ball. When possible, the man with the ball is given the whole side of the court to himself so that he may use one-on-one tactics to keep the ball or break free for a sure shot.

When we are putting on a complete freeze, no shot will be taken or attempted unless the man with the ball is in position to make an uncontested lay-up. The formation employed sets up with two men out and two men in with the big man deploying along the baseline, prepared to break out for a safety pass in case one of his teammates runs into trouble. The four men handling the ball should be the best dribblers and passers and should be drilled in the maneuver until it comes natural for them to dribble, pass, and go away from the receiver.

There are several other methods that can be employed to freeze the ball. All are good. One freeze style, for example, spaces four men along the baseline and permits the team's expert dribbler to work one-on-one against his individual opponent. Another places the two tallest and slowest men on the team in the right and left corners and leaves the ball in the hands of the three best passers who pass and cut *away* from one another so that the man with the ball is always alone on one side of the court, while his two teammates maneuver and keep their opponents busy on the opposite side of the court.

Chart 72

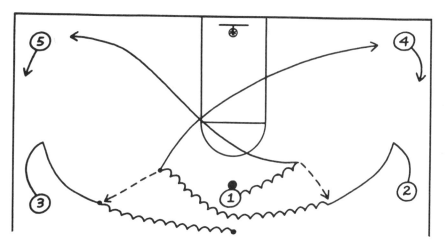

FREEZING TIPS

1. *Keep the area in front of the basket open at all times.*

2. *Always cut away from the teammate to whom you pass the ball.*

3. *When you do not have the ball and are advancing up the sidelines keep faking a change-up for the basket.*

4. *Keep the ball out of the four corners (backcourt and front-court).*

5. *Dribble as little as possible.*

6. *No cross-court or lateral passes. Keep in mind that this is the most dangerous pass in the game. An interception is a sure basket for the opponents.*

7. *Keep moving but hug the baseline in the corner, the side-lines, and the ten-second line. (Always cut toward the basket a short distance from the ten-second line so that you will not receive the ball so close to the line that you have no room to maneuver.)*

8. *Meet the ball at all times. Don't stand and expect the ball to get to you. Remember the opponent is interception-minded.*

9. *No long passes. They are just as dangerous as the cross-court pass.*

10. *Keep away from the teammate with the ball. Give him room to maneuver and dribble. Go to him when it appears he needs your help.*

11. *Keep in mind you are playing out the clock. You are not trying to score.*

12. *No shot will be tried unless it is a lay-up and almost impossible to miss and there is no opponent near the play.*

MEETING THE PRESS

There are so many variations of the press that it is almost impossible to prepare a team to meet all types. However, for the purposes of this book they may be classified as the man-to-man and the zone. In meeting the press (zone, man-to-man, or a variation) a planned and practiced attack should be so thoroughly mastered that the players are ready and able to put the proper maneuvers into immediate use. At South Carolina University we feel that a good dribbler is the key to an attack against any form of the press. In order to give him room to operate successfully, the offense should be spread. With plenty of room to maneuver, the dribbler will be able to use his one-on-one ability to advance the ball. If the backcourt area is congested, the dribbler will have difficulty avoiding possible double-teaming by the opponents.

Besides having a planned and practiced attack against the press it is important that the players be mentally prepared to feel confident of their ability to handle the situation. Assigned positions, duties, practice, and the players' own use of the press will strengthen their con-

Chart 73

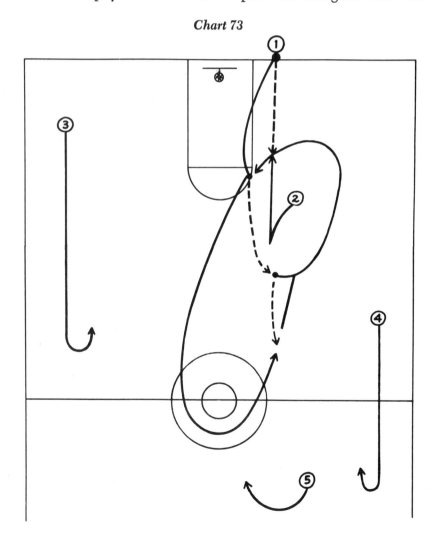

fidence in their ability to handle the situation. And, if they are re-
minded from time to time that their basic offenses enable them to work
through zones and man-to-man defenses in one half of the court, they
will realize that advancing the ball when the opponents are attempting
to guard all over the court is comparatively easy.

In the attack against the press shown by Chart 73, player 1 passes
to teammate 2 who breaks directly back to the ball. Player 1 cuts
straight upcourt and then reverses to receive the ball from teammate 2.
Player 2 then cuts straight upcourt and reverses for the return pass.
Players 3, 4, and 5 are prepared to help out in case they are needed.

In Chart 74 player 1 passes to teammate 3 instead of to player 2
as formerly. Player 1 follows his pass and then angles left upcourt.
Player 3 passes to teammate 2 who has cut ahead of the ball. Player 3
changes direction and cuts ahead of teammate 1. Teammate 1 passes
the ball ahead to teammate 3. Player 3 passes ahead to teammate 2 and

Chart 74

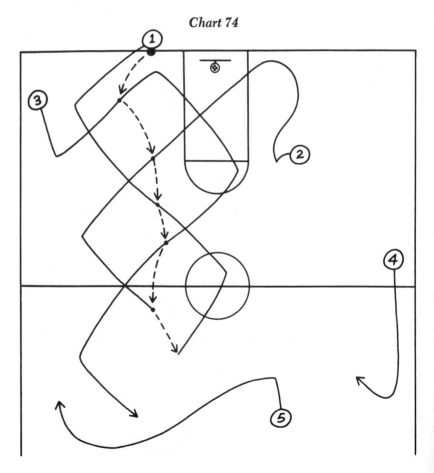

the passing continues until the press retreats. Players 4 and 5 are ready to break to the ball if they are needed.

ATTACKING THE SAG AND THE FLOAT

The sag and the float are employed today to such an extent that it can be safely said that all teams use zone principles in their man-to-man defense. Most of our plays are basically the one-on-one, the two-man give-and-go, and the three-man type. This means that two of our players are comparatively free.

Since the one-, two-, or three-man plays are usually on one side of the court, the opponents often attempt to sag and float away from the free players or away from the weak side of the court (opposite to the side on which the play is being attempted).

We try to take care of these weak-side floaters and front-line saggers by requiring our free players to interchange positions and employ cutting fakes to keep their opponents busy. When the interchanging does not work, we set up screen and block plays against the opponents who are sagging or floating.

In Chart 75 players 1, 2, and 3 are working a play on the right side of the court. Opponents D and E are sagging and floating away from players 4 and 5.

In Chart 76 player 1 passes to teammate 2 and reverses to set an inside screen between teammate 4 and his opponent D (the sagger). Player 2 passes the ball to the big man 3 who dribbles across the lane

Chart 75

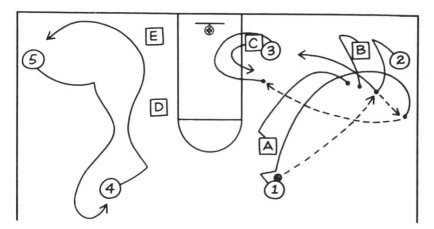

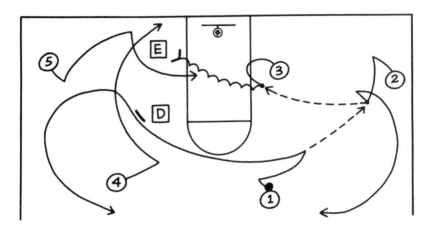

Chart 76

and sets a block behind teammate 5's opponent (the floater), defensive player *E*. Players 4 and 5 cut as shown and should be able to evade their opponents because of the screen and block.

ATTACKING DEFENSIVE VARIATIONS

This book is not large enough to discuss and diagram all the defensive combinations and variations. The combinations range from front-line man-to-man with a back-line zone defense to four-man zones with the remaining player playing a specific attacking opponent on a man-to-man basis.

The screen-switch defense in which defensive players change or switch opponents every time the attacking players cross must be included in these combination defenses, as must those defenses in which four men play man-to-man and one man (usually a tall, agile player) plays a one-man zone. With a few adjustments, the basic offenses that have been outlined can be employed against any of these combinations and variations.

When the front line of the defense plays man-to-man and the rear line plays zone, it is perhaps best to direct the offense against the front-line players, attempting to outnumber the man-to-man opponents, since the back-line zone players will be anchored because of their rebound responsibilities. Naturally, the attack should be directed against the back line should the front line be playing zone and the back line man-to-man.

When the back-line players are using zone principles, it is often possible to use them as blocking posts and attempt to drive their teammates (the players using man-to-man tactics) into the blocks. One of the remaining offensive players should operate behind the back zone line and the other should be used to assist in outnumbering the front-line man-to-man opponents.

The screen-switch defense is often used as a basic team defense. However, some teams restrict the use of the switch to the front-line defensive players. At any rate, the principles used to attack the front line also apply to the back line.

In Chart 77 offensive player 4 is being guarded on a man-to-man basis by defensive player *D*. Instead of trying to score, player 4 works as a passer or to cut behind the zone while his teammates attack the four-man zone box which is set up around the free-throw lane. A simple but excellent play is shown here. Player 1 dribbles slightly to the right to draw opponent *B* away from the big man 3 so he can make sure of the pass. As soon as player 3 receives the ball, he whirls as shown and dribbles down the lane. He can stop and attempt a jump shot from the center of the lane or pass to teammates 2 or 5 who will cut behind the player who attempts to stop his shot. Player 4 keeps his opponent on the move and can move behind teammates 1, 2, and 5 so they will have a positive screen over which to attempt a set shot.

Against the switching defense a change of direction is most effective. It may be included in a roll offense, the five-man give-and-go weave, or the Two-Three offense. In Chart 78 player 1 passes to teammate 2 and starts a screen between 2 and his opponent *B*. Just as

Chart 77

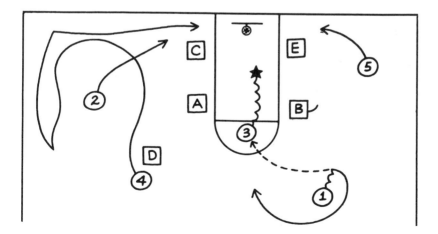

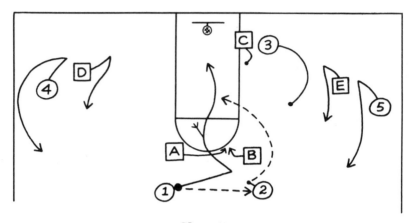

Chart 78

player 1 reaches the point of entry into the inside screen, he changes direction and cuts down the middle of the lane. The big man 3 rolls away from the basket prepared for a pass should his opponent C switch to pick up player 1.

In Chart 79 the defensive players A and B are playing against offensive players 1 and 2 on a man-to-man basis. The other defensive players, C, D, and E, are using zone tactics to take care of the back-line defense. Player 1 passes to teammate 4 and cuts to the left to clear his opponent from the play. Player 4 dribbles to the right, passes to teammate 2, and reverses. Player 2 dribbles sharply toward the basket. Defensive players C and E will have to cover players 4, 3, or 5. One of the three should be open for a pass.

Chart 79

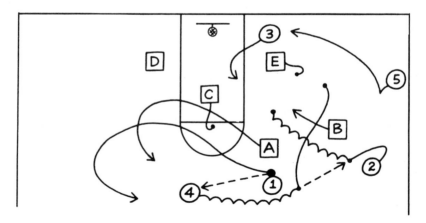

6

defensive philosophies
and principles

A DEFENSIVE PHILOSOPHY

During the past decade the offense has outstripped the defense—
chiefly because of the development of player shooting accuracy and
modern coaching techniques. The high-scoring game is more attractive
to the player and to the fan than the defensive game. So, most players
and coaches concentrate on offensive skills and neglect the defense.

Better facilities, more spacious fieldhouses and gymnasiums, highly
specialized coaching, a greater number of participants, and the all-
around improved physical development of the youth of the country have
resulted in a tremendous number of fine players. This abundance has,
in turn, increased the stature of the game.

In trying to cope with the effectiveness of the various offenses,
coaches now utilize certain offensive and defensive strategies. Offensively, they play possession, control, and stall basketball. Defensively,
they adopt the man-to-man defense with such variations as sagging and
floating and every type of zone application imaginable. In addition, all
types of the press as well as combinations of man-to-man and zone defenses are applied.

111

The result has been a great matching of wits, the defensive coach trying to counter the various offenses in a way that will force his opponent to resort to a weaker or less familiar attack.

Most coaches will agree that a team soundly coached defensively will play a more consistent game than the team coached purely from the offensive point of view. Slowing down a fast-breaking team, keeping the ball away from high-scoring opponents by means of possession basketball, and employing an aggressive, tight, man-to-man defense has often resulted in victory for an apparently overmatched team.

When on the road, a team often develops a case of jitters, finds itself handicapped by officiating interpretations, the strange floor, baskets, and lighting, and an unfriendly crowd reaction, with the result that the club's offense has an "off" night. However, most coaches would agree that a team defense seldom has an off night. All coaches are looking constantly for a good defensive player who can black-out the opposing team's star. Not infrequently, when the coach or a fan sums up a game by saying, "We were off in our shooting," he really means that the defense set up by the opponents was too tough for his team.

The importance of defense

All coaches like to teach and supervise offensive drills. The players like offensive play—will run and shoot and cut and dribble and screen and fast-break with everything they have. But when it comes to defensive drills, the coach finds that not only do the players experience a letdown, but that he also loses a lot of enthusiasm.

Here, it is the job of the coach to attack the defensive problems and drills with enthusiasm; to sell his players on the importance of this phase of the game. Some coaches begin their early season practice with defensive work, holding out offensive drills and plays as an incentive for good work in the defensive side of the game.

When it comes to making a choice between the use of the press, the man-to-man, the zone, or some combination of these, as the team defense, the experience of the coach and the quality of the players (experience and physical abilities) must govern the selection. It is probably true that the man-to-man defense is considered the basic defense by the majority of coaches. And, most coaches would agree that the press works best off the man-to-man. The use of the press as a basic defense will, undoubtedly, result in higher scoring—not only for the pressing team but for the opponents as well. The use of the zone as a basic defense will certainly slow down the attack of the opponents and their scoring total. And, because of the advantage which is present when it is made from the zone, a fast-break offense would probably increase the scoring total of the team using the zone.

At any rate, the selection of the basic defense to be used, and the addition of the supporting measures with which to strengthen the basic defense, is an important part of the science of coaching. The coach should probably devote more time to the determination of his defense and its supporting measures than to his offense.

Basketball players today are such fine marksmen that, more than ever before, the old basketball axiom that the best defense is a good offense seems to be applicable. However, there must be some semblance of balance between offense and defense, or basketball becomes merely a game of individual skills. It is understandable that the development of an offense is more fun, but there is much more of a challenge to be found in the building of a good defense or defenses.

Good defense is consistent

When a coach prepares his team to meet all possible offensive situations, he can approach each game with a feeling of confidence. He knows that his team will be a strong opponent even when his players are off in their shooting or passing, are faced with a tight defense, or meet a better offensive team. Away from home, floors, baskets, lighting, officials (presently approaching uniformity throughout the country), and crowd reaction usually handicap the offense. However, a strong defense is almost as effective on one court as another and will provide the team time in which to adjust its offense to the surroundings.

Psychologically, a strong defense places an immediate burden upon the opponents. They feel called upon for a special effort; they are cautious and constantly on the alert for some sort of surprise strategy. This limits their usual freedom in attacking—an advantage, of course, to the defensive team.

Many teams have earned great defensive reputations by playing control basketball and keeping the ball away from their opponents. Today, all players are shooters; they are anxious to score; they want the ball. Players who can keep the ball, who can control the natural urge to score, and who wait for a free and open shot at the basket will control the score by keeping the ball away from their opponents. And, quite often, a stronger team will be defeated by an inferior one that has mastered ball-control and self-control.

All offensive and sharpshooting teams have bad nights, nights when the players can't even throw the ball into the ocean. When this occurs, the high-scoring team that has developed a strong defensive game can fall back on this important asset and may pull out of the fire a game that might easily have been lost.

It is important to keep in mind that there is an offensive saturation point beyond which a team can seldom rise. Much of the time spent in offensive work could be put to far better use in developing a good, strong defense.

Surprise strategy may take many forms. It may be a change in offensive tactics through elimination of the fast break and freedom shooting and the adoption of a possession offense. An opponent geared to match a hard-running, fast-breaking, free-shooting and high-scoring team may be completely upset by the opponents' use of a stall offense. Offensive surprises often succeed in upsetting certain opponents, but it is the surprise defense that is most likely to be encountered.

High school teams and defense

For many years, high school coaches have maintained that the college coach could resort to the use of varied defenses in his coaching because of the advanced players on hand. That philosophy has been exploded time and again by championship high school teams who have mixed up their defenses—not only from game to game, but many times in a single game.

It is not uncommon at present for certain high school teams to employ a tight, man-to-man defense that uses the switch, sagging, floating, player-overshifting, and collapsing-rebound methods. In addition, many of these fine high school teams may change from man-to-man to one type of zone; then to another; then to a half-, three-quarter, or full-court press. Going further, some of these wonderfully coached teams may even use a combination of the man-to-man and the zone defense (the front line applying tight, man-to-man tactics with the rear line—usually three players—using some form of zone formation or vice versa).

There are hundreds of defensive possibilities as yet unexplored in the game of basketball. Most coaches spend 75 per cent of practice time developing individual and team offensive skills and the rest of the period in defensive work. With the offense developed to a high point of efficiency, it is not surprising that coaches are turning more and more to the teaching of defensive measures. Right here, it may be pertinent to state that the use of multiple defensive systems is not in itself enough to guarantee success. Performance is the test. If the players feel that the opponents will be upset simply because of a change from a man-to-man to some type of the zone or other surprise defense, then the coach is wasting his time.

Hard, undiluted work is required in applying any defense. There is no easy defense. The old axiom that the player should relax on the offense but never on the defense is still pertinent. There is no substitute for effort, for aggressive, tenacious, determined, defensive *work*.

A DEFENSIVE CODE

A code is sometimes defined as a comprehensive and systematic body of principles or rules ascertained by experience and governing procedures in force within a certain scope. As a high school, college, and professional player and later as a high school and college coach, I have formulated a defensive code which has been based upon playing and coaching experience. It is not surprising, therefore, that I have adopted certain defensive principles which I feel are necessary in developing a strong defense. It is necessary to start with the player and then move on to the defensive principles.

The player is the essence. The development of a defense starts with the abilities of the squad as individuals and as a group. The high school coach must start with boys who have had little or no defensive training; thus he has an opportunity to "start them right." In the writer's opinion, boys should be taught man-to-man principles as the fundamental base upon which to build all types of team defenses. No matter what team defense the boy may be called upon to play later—man-to-man, zone, screen-switch, combination, or variation—each will require application of man-to-man principles.

Summing up the above, the use of various defenses is desirable, but variety alone does not guarantee effectiveness. The success of any type of defense depends on the players' application of the various parts. One player slacking off will weaken the entire structure. Quite often the star offensive player slacks off in defensive work to such an extent that his value to the team as a whole is questionable. A strong, devoted defensive substitute may insure victory even though he does not score a single point. Naturally, the good defensive team is the one that has been grounded thoroughly in the basic parts of the man-to-man defense. Once the players have mastered good man-to-man defensive play, development and application of multiple defenses may be approached with confidence.

Man-to-man is basic defense

At South Carolina University all freshmen are required to learn the man-to-man defense. In this connection, I feel that grade school, club, junior high, high school, and college freshmen players should be prohibited from use of zone defenses and other combinations before they have mastered the man-to-man defense.

All boys are individualists and must be treated as such. It is up to the coach to reach each of his players through the medium of a challenge, through pride, or by acclaim. Once a player grasps the principles of the man-to-man defense and applies them in actual scrimmage, he begins to see the light and develops a feeling of pride in his defensive ability.

The South Carolina University freshman team uses a straight man-to-man defense. Whenever possible the players are matched according to height, weight, speed, and fundamental defensive abilities and skills. Then they are expected to employ good defensive positions, use hands and feet correctly, and observe the in-line principle.

When front, slide, stay, and switch have been drilled until they become second nature, and when blocking-out and rebounding techniques are in good shape, we turn to such variations or additions as overshifting, sagging, floating, closing the gate, and offensive, absolute, and collapsing defenses.

Our varsity players utilize all of the man-to-man principles but we continue to drill them again and again until the moves and reactions are automatically applied in any given defensive situation.

When we are satisfied that the team's application of the straight man-to-man defense can be applied tightly to any attack, we move on to a distinction between offensive and defensive defense. When an offensive defense is being used, the front-line players are expected to take chances, to break frequently while the opponents' shot is in the air, and to ignore blocking-out responsibilities. Naturally, these variations are used only when our deep men are capable of handling the defensive backboard assignment without help from the front-line players.

When a defensive defense (absolute) is being used, all players are responsible for blocking out. The front-line players are expected to collapse after blocking out and every player concentrates on getting the ball. No thought whatever is given to utilization of the fast break when the absolute defense is in operation.

The defensive break, or the shift from offense to defense, is of utmost importance. Good offensive court balance while attacking is the first step in this vital move. Hustle and team realization of the necessity of a fast retreat to help out are difficult to teach, but the rewards are great.

After the team has mastered the basic man-to-man defense, we familiarize each man with several zone defenses. A particular zone may be used when scouting or other information indicates the opponent may not be able to cope with this type of defense. Combinations of man-to-man and zone defenses are frequently effective against certain teams. Although we do not specialize in these combinations, we have used and will continue to use any defense that we think will help us win games.

Each player must do his job

We start every game with a personal match-up. Scouting reports give us information about the individual strengths and weaknesses of each opponent. Using this information, we assign (match up) players to particular opponents on the basis of height, speed, weight, and other characteristics. If each of our players does his job, we will have a good defense for the game. Adjustments must be made after the game starts, of course. We try to anticipate these moves in order to make them without taking a time out. For example, we may have to change a match-up or double-team some opponent who gets very hot.

If our defense needs tightening up, we may make changes in the lineup, putting particularly strong defensive players into the game even if the offensive strength is weakened. Of course, this will depend upon the score and other game factors.

By the time our first game of the season rolls around, our team is prepared to "close the gate"; play the opponents loose and jam the middle area if they have no effective outside shooters; use the sag and the float to combat a driving attack; use a zone to meet a driving weave or a roll offense; and employ some form of the press when the opponents are too big for us or are poor ball handlers.

7

man-to-man
team defense

DEFENSIVE TEAM PRINCIPLES

With the individual skills mastered, the next job in building a team defense is to coordinate them with several broad defensive team principles.

Four basic principles

First in importance is court and defensive balance. Court and defensive balance begins while the team is in possession of the ball in its front court and is applying an offense. The basic circulation must be thoroughly mastered to insure backcourt coverage at all times. Constant warnings about maintaining defensive balance while working on team offenses are necessary to stress the importance of this principle. The coach should not hesitate to stop the workout or scrimmage whenever this defensive coverage is found missing. Backcourt players must accept responsibility by calling corner teammates back to help out when help is needed.

Second, retreating methods (shifting from the offensive court to the defensive court) must be checked again and again to make sure that the players are trained to pick up loose opponents. When picking up, the first player back on the defense should direct the defense, assigning teammates to opponents according to their proximity to the basket. In addition, this first-player-back should adjust the retreat to various attacks.

Third, there must be a thorough team understanding and application of the in-line principle and complete realization of the importance of playing as a unit; the necessity of talking: "Watch the pick!" "Stay!" "Slide!" "Switch!" "Hands up!"

The fourth necessity is the ability to take advantage of match-ups so that overshifting, use of the sag and the float, and closing-the-gate principles may be utilized. The team then should be prepared to meet the threat of the big man, employ an offensive, loose, collapsible (absolute) defense, and stop the opponents' fast break.

Ability to meet the freeze, apply the press, and defend against the various game situations must be developed before the team advances to zone and combination defenses.

Defensive areas

Setting up defensive areas and deciding how far from the basket the front line of defense should be established is also important. Chart 80 shows the defensive zones. In connection with these zones a set of principles has been designed to provide rules for the players.

Chart 80

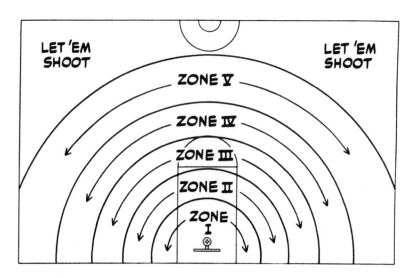

DEFENSIVE AREAS

Zone 1. Play in front of the post-pivot man. Form defensive triangle here. When opponent is lost, head first for this zone. Jam it up! "No cheap baskets permitted."

Zone 2. Second most important defensive zone. Play aggressive defense. Switch on a post-pivot pass of the ball. Attempt to stop all shots taken. Talk! Use slide, front, and switch. Play the man first, attempt interceptions second.

Zone 3. This is the third most important defensive zone. Play behind post-pivot opponent. Give him a little more room so teammates can slide through. In this zone use the sag and the float when away from the ball. Intercept the ball if you can. Be aggressive and a tough defensive man here. Anticipate passes.

Zone 4. Loosen up defense a bit except against player with ball. Sag and float in this zone. Fight through screens. Play your own man and forget the switch unless it is absolutely necessary; the switch must be called by the defensive player in on the screen or block who is closest to the defensive basket. Don't play opponent too tight unless he has the ball.

Zone 5. Danger points in this zone are in the corners and straight down the middle. Cover these three areas closely. Close the gate and play them loose in other parts of this zone. If poor outside shooters don't play tight, clog the middle and the zone area from the sidelines in to the lane.

Let them shoot from the "coffin corners" unless in the final seconds and behind in the score.

Scouting information and the trend of the actual game may necessitate the use of several variations in the straight man-to-man defense. Certain opponent teams may include excellent set shooters who are accurate outside scorers. These opponents must be played closely in Zone 4 and frequently in Zone 5.

Other teams may drive consistently for the basket and may be adept at screening and blocking so that they can free a teammate for a clear shot in Zone 1 or 2. This may call for the use of the switch on every ball play and for considerable sagging and floating to jam these two under-basket zones.

The opponents may feature a strong, high-scoring post-pivot player who is so dangerous in Zones 1 and 2 that the defensive big man may not be able to cope with him without help from teammates. In this case it may be necessary to sacrifice the defense in Zones 3 and 4 to get help in the under-basket area through sagging and floating.

Another team may feature a strong follow-in attack requiring the use of all defensive players under the basket, blocking out and retreating in an attempt to secure the rebound.

When the straight man-to-man defense, with or without the use of the switch and sagging and floating, is not strong enough to cope with the opponents, it may be necessary to shift to a combination defense or one of the zone defenses.

Defensive court balance

Defensive court balance is fairly easy to develop when a weave or roll circulation is employed in the offense. When the give-and-go, slicing plays, and a driving attack are used, defensive balance is difficult to maintain. A strong quarterback who possesses good leadership and court savvy is undoubtedly the key here, since he is usually instrumental in setting up the attack and can foresee the need for help in the backcourt.

Chart 81 illustrates defensive court balance. Player 1 (the quarterback) passes the ball to teammate 2 and starts for the corner. Player 2 passes the ball to the right corner man 3 and, at the same time, backcourt 4 cuts for the basket. Player 1 realizes that the backcourt will be left without defensive balance (at least two men required) and retreats as shown. He then calls upon the left corner man (5) to help him set up the backcourt defensive balance.

Chart 81

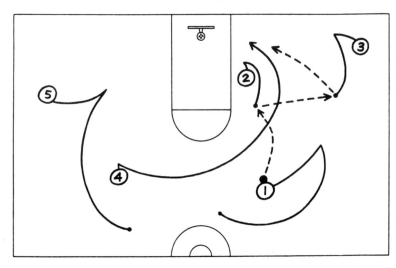

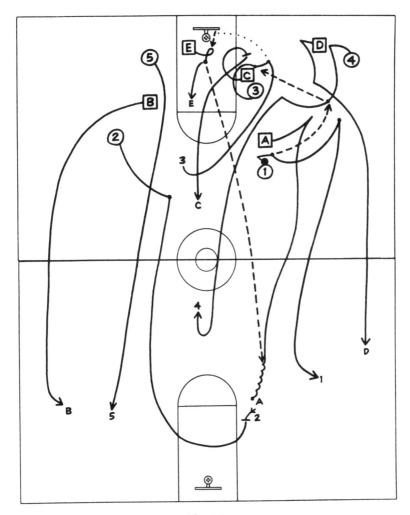

Chart 82

Chart 82 illustrates a retreating defense. Offensive player 1 passes to the right corner man 4 and cuts toward the right sideline. The corner man 4 passes the ball to the big man 3 who has circled to a scoring position on the right side of the lane. Player 3 shoots and the rebound is taken by opponent E who sets himself for a long pass to A. Opponents A and B have instituted a break with the shot and defensive player 1 is caught out of position.

The offense is now changing to defense and player 2 assumes the defensive quarterback duties. He points to opponent A and calls out that he will cover him. He then directs his teammates 1 and 5 to cover opponents D and B respectively. Player 2 then proceeds to try to stop the dribbler as shown. In the meantime, teammate 4 has retreated and is set to pick up opponent C. He (4) now yells to the big man (teammate 3) to trade opponents and pick up E.

Retreating methods

Years ago, the standing guard was a bulwark of the defense. He was usually restricted to the backcourt and relied upon a long set shot for his scoring. His primary responsibility was to see that the defense was assembled when the opponents got the ball. Secondarily he was used as a safety player to whom the ball could be returned when the offense faltered. Some coaches still rely upon this backcourt operator to take care of the defense.

Modern offenses and the high scoring load carried by backcourt players have practically put the standing guard out of business. Teams now retreat more or less as a unit unless caught in a surprise fast-break situation. Even then, there is a team reaction which calls for an orderly retreat and an efficient picking up of opponents.

When a backcourt player is caught all alone by a quick advance of opponents, he tries to hold the fort until help arrives. If it is a three-on-one or a two-on-one situation, he fakes from player to player with the progress of the ball until he is under the basket. Here, he can only continue to fake coverage of the opponent with the ball until help arrives.

If the two backcourt players are opposed by a three-on-two situation, they employ the defensive shuttle until help can arrive.

DEFENSIVE TEAM VARIATIONS

Any deviation from the straight in-line man-to-man defense may properly be called a variation. Naturally, these variations are a compromise between the straight in-line observance of the man-to-man defense and the usual zone principles. Overshifting, switching, sagging, floating, playing in front of the opponent close to the basket, concentrating on the ball while still playing an assigned opponent, collapsing to the under-basket area, and massing in the close scoring zones, are all variations of the man-to-man defense and are all popular in team defenses.

Use of stay, front, slide, back, and switch is fairly common, and these variations are necessary in coping with the effectiveness of the various screens and blocks in use.

The screen-switch defense, adopted to counter the effectiveness of screens and blocks, incorporates man-to-man and zone principles. Switching by defensive players places them in more favorable guarding positions, and the elimination of assigned-man responsibility enables them to concentrate upon interceptions and the fast break.

Sagging and floating

Sagging and floating enable players to use zone principles and still observe their man-to-man assignments. Because the sagging and floating players may leave their assigned opponents when the offense is centered in another area, the defensive team can set up a zone concentration in the all-important scoring area near the basket.

Team use of sagging and floating closely resembles the movement of players employing the zone defense. The chief difference is that the assigned-man principle remains in effect.

Sagging and floating lends itself efficiently to such team defensive maneuvers as closing the gate, collapsing for team rebounding, massing in the cutting and scoring lanes against the opponents' set attack as well as against held-ball and out-of-bounds situations. Not only does the sagging and floating discourage cutting by opponents but it sets up a threat against passes into the area.

Combination defenses are covered in detail in Chapter 9 of this book. Here we intend only to draw attention to the fact that man-to-man and zone principles are utilized in setting up varying lines of defense. The man-to-man principle may be in effect in the front line of the defense and the zone principle in the back line or vice versa. Such combinations often change in character with the movement of the ball into different areas.

Closing the gate

When the opponents are expert in the use of the give-and-go and in driving or dribbling down the center of the court or toward the lane

Chart 83

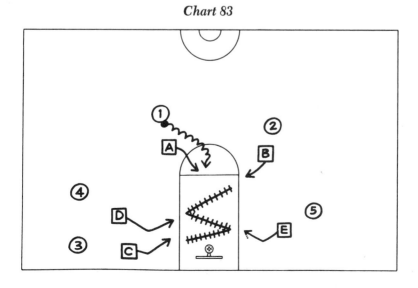

from the side of the court, the sag or the float or both may be combined to close the gate. The players must be drilled in this variation until they can close the gate and immediately spring back to the in-line position when the maneuver is completed.

In Chart 83 offensive player 1 dribbles down the center of the lane closely guarded by defensive *A*. Defensive players *B*, *D*, *C*, and *E* join in helping their teammate *A* by sagging and floating toward the lane to close the gate.

TEAM PROBLEM OF THE BIG MAN

Extending the width of the free-throw line to 12 feet has partially checked the scoring potential of the big man, but defensing him is just as difficult. The good, big man can ruin you with his shooting, rebounding, or feeding the cutters (to say nothing of his screening and blocking value).

By defensing the big man, we mean defending the under-basket area against any man. The trend today is for any of three men to play the post-pivot position, moving from the corners or from the sides of the court. Some teams employ the double pivot, thus placing a heavier burden on the defense. What can be done to defense the big man (or big men) in the under-basket zone? First of all, in most situations, it is advisable to play your own biggest man against him. With this in mind, the following strategies are suggested:

BIG MAN STRATEGY ALTERNATIVES

1. *Play between the ball and the pivot player.*

2. *Play the pivot man three-quarters.*

3. *Double-team the pivot man.*

4. *Use a collapsing defense to surround the pivot man.*

5. *Use a zone defense or a combination defense.*

6. *Apply the full-court press.*

Defensively, the big man must be able to carry his share of the load. Championship teams and championship contenders usually feature a big man who presents a defensive problem. The opponents' big man must be met on even terms. Your own big man should be prepared to play the opposing giant from behind, on the side, or in front, and should have the ability to keep up with him in the corners or out on the court.

Chart 84 illustrates a big-man defense that involves playing in front and cross-check. Defensive player *C* is playing in front of the big man, opponent 3, with the express purpose of playing between 3 and the ball. Here, offensive player 1 passes the ball to his teammate 3 by means of a high, loop pass. Defensive player *C* extends his hands above his head hoping to deflect the ball as he turns with opponent 3. If he is

Chart 84

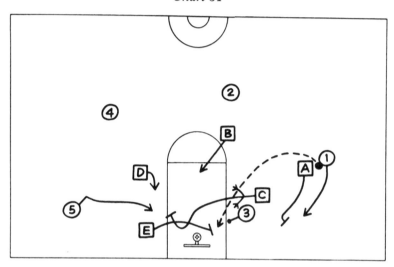

Chart 85

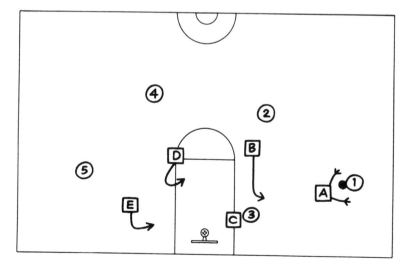

unsuccessful in deflecting the ball, he will cross over to switch opponents with teammate *E* who has cut across the lane to cover 3 and attempt to intercept the ball. This cross-check is used by all first-class man-to-man defense teams.

Chart 85 illustrates double-teaming the big man. Here, defensive player *B* has dropped back in front of the big man 3 to discourage the pass from opponent 1 to opponent 3. Other players are dropping back to congest the lane area.

Playing between the ball and the man

The best way of playing a high-scoring pivot man who sets up underneath is from the front. The important thing is to prevent him from getting the ball while in good shooting position. Once he does, it becomes practically impossible to control his hook, turn, and jump shots.

Playing in front of the pivot man makes it extremely tough to get the ball in to him. The smart front-playing guard will keep his hands up and moving and avoid turning his head to locate his man. He may watch the pivot with split vision or with darting glances out of the corners of his eyes (when possible).

A tall, agile, alert defensive man who keeps his hands up can put a severe crimp in the pivot man's scoring. If the latter can't get the ball, he can't score and will be forced to come out to a higher post—which is what you want him to do.

When the big man starts to figure-eight under the boards, he becomes difficult to guard. Nevertheless, it's still best to try to stay in front of him or at least at his side as he makes this maneuver.

Playing the pivot man three-quarters

It has been a standard practice at South Carolina University to play the pivot man three-quarters—though we prefer our man in front if he can do it. By "three-quarters" is meant playing the pivot on the (ball) side and nearly in front, with the hand extended in front to intercept the pass or at least make it tough to get through. From this three-quarters stance, the defensive pivot man can also circle his man and keep in continuous movement to hinder his efficiency.

Double-teaming

The strategy of double-teaming is often possible when the opponents do not shoot enough from the outside to force front-line players to stay up on them. One of the front-line players can drop back to a position where he can intercept a direct pass to the big man. The player defending the big man drops behind him. The use of the Two-One-Two zone will also permit the use of this double-teaming principle. The front-line player who is not guarding the man with the ball will drop back in front of the big opponent, and the back-line player will play behind him.

Using a collapsing defense

When using the man-to-man defense, it is possible to have the player guarding the outside feeder drop off him and get in front of the pivot man, while our big man will play in back of him. We also have our weak-side defensive player come over and help out from his side of the court. This places three men on our opponents' big man.

Using a zone defense

On occasions we use the One-Three-One defensive zone originated by Clair Bee. The principle involved here is to keep three players between the ball and the basket at all times. This makes it virtually impossible to work the ball into the pivot man. Although this defense is weak against good outside shooters, it's excellent against a team with a dominant scorer in the under-basket area.

The full-court press

The full-court press can be defined as a defense in which opponents are aggressively guarded as soon as they obtain the ball in their rear court. The opportunity to apply a full-court press would, therefore, follow a successful or unsuccessful attempt to score, a rebound, interception, or pass into the court from out-of-bounds.

A full-court press may be applied with man-to-man or zone techniques, the objective being to force the opponents to play under pressure in a different manner from their accustomed style; to prevent the big boy from getting into his favorite spot under the boards; and to make it difficult for the offense to advance the ball across the ten-second line within the time limit. The press often forces the big man to set up a post far from his basket in order to help his team to advance the ball into the front court within ten seconds.

The full-court press can be highly effective against a team with an outstanding scoring pivot man, because it keeps him from securing his favorite scoring position near the basket. And, when the opponents have two or three big men, the full-court press may exert terrific pressure on the smaller backcourt men who are bringing the ball upcourt. Further, since most big men aren't used to bringing the ball upcourt, if the full-court press can force them to do so occasionally, it may result in interceptions, charging fouls, fumbles, and loss of the ball.

SPECIAL MAN-TO-MAN TEAM DEFENSES

Offensive defense

When the backboard can be controlled by the big men without help from the front-line defensive players, an offensive defense may be used. This means that the front-line players may break immediately for their basket when opponents attempt a shot. This is possible because they are secure in the knowledge that the ball will be safely rebounded. Usually, the coach will restrain this type of break until the ball is actually in possession, having been safely rebounded by one of the back-line rebounders.

Chart 86 shows an offensive defense. Offensive player 1 has taken advantage of a block set by offensive 3 and dribbled to the outer half of the free-throw circle for a shot. Defensive player *A* was blocked and switched to guard opponent 3. However, when he saw opponent 1 take the shot and also saw that his rebounder teammate *E* was in position to successfully rebound the ball, he (*A*) broke for his own basket up the right sideline. Teammate *B* also broke up the middle lane and when *E* passed the ball to *A*, defensive player *C* broke down the left sideline.

Chart 86

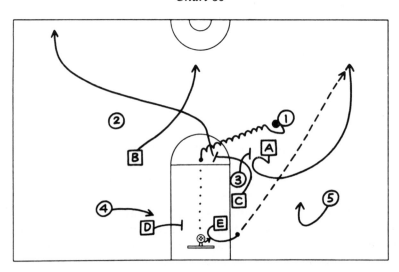

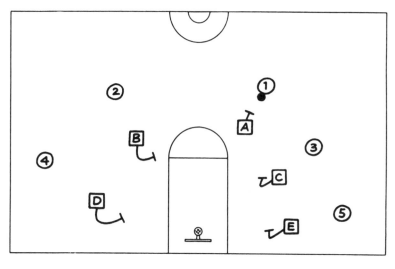

Chart 87

Loose man-to-man defense

A loose man-to-man defense can often be used effectively against a team schooled to work the ball in toward the basket for close shots. The spacing between the defensive players and their opponents lessens as the defense is forced back toward the basket. This loose defense is also an excellent type to use against give-and-go tactics, hard cutters, and a slicing offense.

Chart 87 shows a loose man-to-man defense. Defensive players A, B, C, D, and E are playing their opponents 1, 2, 3, 4, and 5, loosely. Since the defense is being applied because the opponents are poor outside shooters, screens, picks, and blocks for outside shots are possible. However, the loose guarding almost entirely eliminates screens, setscreens, picks, and blocks close to the basket.

COLLAPSING MAN-TO-MAN DEFENSE

The collapsing man-to-man defense employed at South Carolina University consists of sagging and floating away from opponents whenever the ball is in play in another area. As soon as the players realize the collapsing defense is in effect, they are expected to use sagging and floating principles at every opportunity. The team sagging and floating usually places our defensive players in a position where they can jam the middle and help with the team rebounding.

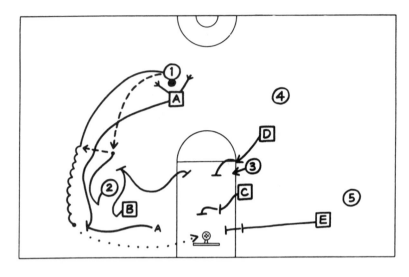

Chart 88

The opponent with the ball is played tightly and with one hand held up above the ball. We use the expression "hand above the ball" to imply that the man with the ball could not shoot it or that the shot would be considered a forced shot if he did succeed in getting it away.

Chart 88 shows a collapsing man-to-man defense. Offensive player 1 passes the ball to his teammate 2 and cuts to the right. Player 2 returns the ball to 1 who dribbles toward the baseline and attempts a shot. As soon as the shot is attempted, defensive players *A, B, C, D,* and *E* collapse toward the basket making sure that no offensive opponent breaks through. When the ball rebounds, all five of the defensive players concentrate on getting possession of the ball. No thought of the fast break is in the minds of the defensive players; possession of the ball is paramount.

Rebounding

In this defense, all players are taught to go to the defensive backboard as soon as a shot is taken. The rebound triangle is first set up and then the free-throw circle area is covered. All players fight for the ball, blocking out opponents when possible to aid a teammate in making the rebound.

The fast break is never used from the collapsing defense. We are more concerned with rebounding and our objective is to control the boards and hold our set attack until we have advanced across the center line and into scoring territory.

The collapsing defense is effective against teams that have a poor reputation as "outside" shooters or who have only one accurate distance marksman. It is also effective against single- or double-pivot offenses.

The principle of "arm's length" is used in guarding opponents with or without the ball on the side of the court where the offensive players are attempting to set up a play. All other defensive players employ sagging and/or floating principles. Freshmen players are taught this defense after they have mastered the in-line principles of the man-to-man defense, but they are not allowed to turn their heads to follow the ball. They are expected to concentrate on their assigned opponents and recover the ball only when it rebounds directly to them. Opponents in the vicinity of the center line are not played unless scouting reports reveal that particular players possess excellent long shots.

STOPPING THE FAST BREAK

The fast break is the stock in trade of all professional basketball teams as well as a great majority of college and high school teams. Before meeting a fast-break team for the first time, it is wise to secure a thorough scouting report, preferably first hand. Few, indeed, are the independent basketball scouts who can give a coach a first-class report upon a rival's fast break and how to meet it in terms of the coach's playing personnel and their abilities. However, there are a number of points a scout may cover which may be valuable in attempting to slow down the opponents' fast break.

The tactics of the offense

First, it is important to know the type of fast break. Is it a planned style based on a particular type? Is it a "freedom" style in which the players take advantage of defensive lapses? Is it limited to passing, dribbling (after the outlet pass), straight lines, or criss-crossing? How is the ball put in to play? From the backboard? From an interception? Following a score from the free-throw line or from the field?

Who puts the ball in play? Does the fast break depend upon the ability of the tall center to get the outlet pass away? Are there other members of the team who assist in getting the ball on its way? Where is the outlet pass usually directed? What is the pattern of the break when it approaches scoring territory? Which players usually score? From what part of the scoring area? What type of shots are attempted?

The tactics of the defense

After the above questions have been answered, they should be broken down and tied in with the abilities of the members of the defensive coach's own team. If the attack is planned, how can it be stopped? If a key player is vital to the break, how can he be checked? Can the big rebounder be pressed? How does he react to pressure? Can the receiver of the outlet pass be pressed? Can the pattern of the attack be disrupted? When the break approaches scoring area can some sort of a defense be applied to check its success? Can one of the defense's backcourt players be assigned to stop the dribbler? Can the other be assigned to concentrate on the fast-break scorer?

If all of these tactics are ineffective, it may be necessary to apply a man-to-man or a zone press. At any rate, it is wise to make some preparation to meet the team with an effective fast break, whether it be attempting to disrupt their plans as outlined above or by slowing down the attack. It may be absolutely necessary to make sure your team's attacking moves are always supported by good defensive balance. This balance may be gained through the medium of good offensive circulation which insures a return to the backcourt by the backcourt players or replacement by one of their frontcourt teammates when the backcourt man cuts through for a scoring play. It may even be necessary to keep two men back at all times, maneuvering carefully on the offense until a good shot is possible. Follow-in tactics might be stressed. Certain men can be definitely assigned the responsibility for this chore, particularly with respect to the opponents' key rebounders.

South Carolina's tactics

At South Carolina University we fall back on the following measures when considering just how we can stop an opponent's fast break. *First*, if the opponents are faster and concentrate on the fast break, we use our possession game to control the ball and keep it away from them by attempting only sure, close-to-the-basket shots.

Second, we make sure that our defensive balance is maintained.

Third, we concentrate on our follow-in tactics. Scouting notes or game observation enable us to determine whether the opponents rely upon one, two, or three rebounders to get possession of the ball to start their offensive run upcourt. Once we know the rebounding strength, we are able to set up a follow-in plan.

Against the average opponent, we try to match their rebound strength with our follow-in strength. In other words, if they rely upon two men to get the ball, we match against these rebounders two of our own follow-in players. If they use the rebound triangle, relying upon three men to get the ball, we send three follow-in players to oppose them.

The matching of follow-in men with the opponents' rebounders enables us also to match the outside players to whom the ball will be passed. If one of these opponents is the fast-break dribbler, one of our backcourt players presses him in an attempt to discourage the rebounder from sending an outlet pass in his direction.

When we attempt a shot, the matching of rebounder against rebounder naturally determines the number of men to set up our defensive balance. The follow-in players make every effort to regain the ball or tap it to their teammates in the backcourt. When the opposing rebounders secure the ball, the follow-in player who is closest to the opponent with the ball plays him aggressively in an attempt to delay the outlet pass. The other follow-in player or players drop back and prepare to pick up the other rebounders as they move downcourt.

The backcourt players who have set up the defensive balance try to cover the outlet-pass areas and pick up their opponents at the same time.

Since most fast-breaking attacks depend upon the use of the dribble after the ten-second line is passed, our next plan is to stop the dribbler. One of our backcourt players picks up the dribbler and falls back, playing dummy until he feels the timing is right. Then, he fakes an interception attempt in an effort to force the dribbler to stop. If he is successful, and the dribbler stops with the ball, the defensive man attempts to tie him up. But if the dribbler tries to go around him, the backcourt player tries to steal the ball, slapping *upward* on the side the dribbler is attacking an attempt to knock the ball away.

In the meantime, the other backcourt player retreats to the under-basket zone and, if outnumbered by a two-on-one situation, tries to get help from a teammate by using the fake and the one-man shuttle. If a teammate arrives and they are outnumbered in a three-on-two situation, they use the two-man shuttle to gain time and attempt to intercept the ball. The shuttle is used only when the under-basket players are outnumbered.

The follow-in players who may have been left behind are expected to retreat at full speed toward their defensive basket and to try to pick up opponents who may attempt the short, outside shot.

In Chart 89 defensive players 1 and 2 wait for the advance and decide upon the start of the shuttle. Player 1 advances to check the dribbler in the outer half of the free-throw area. (1 should not advance farther than the free-throw line.) Player 2 fakes to cover the closest opponent (*C*) and retreats in front of the basket.

In Chart 90 offensive player *A* passes the ball to his teammate *B*. Defensive player 2 immediately covers opponent *B* and defensive player 1 drops back under the basket. (This area is never left open.)

In Chart 91 offensive player *B* passes the ball across to his team-

Chart 89

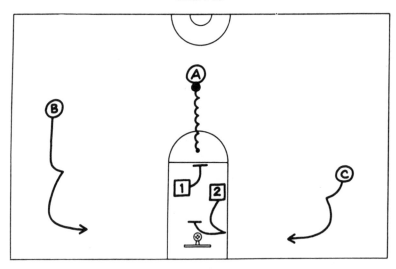

Chart 90

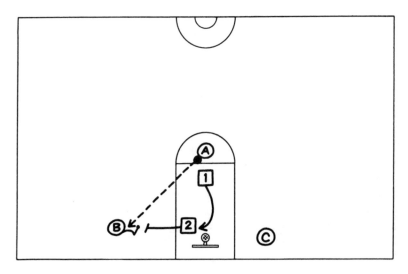

mate (*C*) on the other side of the basket. Defensive player 1 now covers opponent *C* and defensive player 2 covers the under-basket area.

In Chart 92 offensive player *C* passes the ball back to his teammate *A* on the free-throw line. Defensive player 2 immediately covers opponent *A*. Defensive player 1 covers the under-basket area.

In Chart 93 offensive player *A* returns the ball to *C*. Defensive

Chart 91

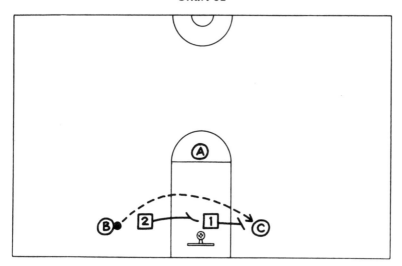

Chart 92

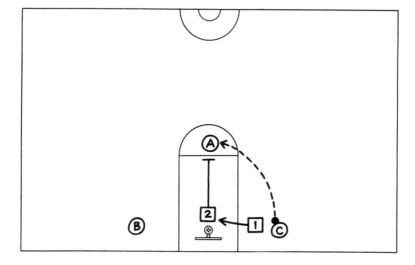

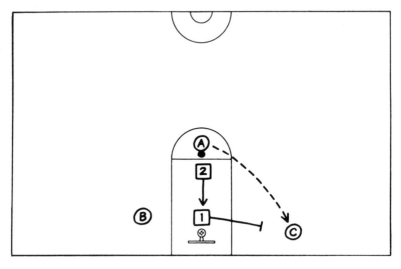

Chart 93

player 1 immediately cover opponent *C* and defensive player 2 retreats to cover the dangerous under-basket area.

ADVANTAGES OF THE MAN-TO-MAN DEFENSE

1. *Players may be matched according to their individual playing and physical abilities.*

2. *It fixes responsibility; the coach and teammates recognize laxity in individual guarding assignments.*

3. *It encourages individual development of personal and team skills.*

4. *It is adaptable to any type of attack, particularly those which employ spread tactics.*

5. *Its use is absolutely imperative in the closing minutes of a game when behind in the score.*

6. *It enables the defense to take advantage of weaknesses of opponents (by floating and sagging and double-teaming).*

7. *It is comparatively simple in principle and application.*

8. *It is the basic defense and its principles, in part, apply to all defenses.*

9. **It permits a wide range of defensive applications to meet the offensive strengths of opponents.**

10. **It lends itself to a great number of variations that are simple and easy to apply.**

SUPPORT MAN-TO-MAN DEFENSE

The support man-to-man defense is most certainly a team defense. In modern-day basketball, it is extremely difficult, if not impossible, for a defensive man to adequately cover an offensive man in a one-on-one situation. We believe each defender must feel (with confidence) that his teammates will support him in case the offensive man makes a good offensive maneuver and thus places his guard at a disadvantage. This confidence in the support of his teammates enables the defensive man covering the opponent with the ball to be more aggressive in his defensive play. This aggressiveness is possibly the best way to cover a good jump shooter.

Terminology varies to describe sloughing, sagging, helping, collapsing, or supporting. We like the terms "supporting" or "helping," as they signify the team's intention to support or help one another and to prevent successfully most good-percentage shots. The support man-to-man defense combines many of the advantages of the man-to-man defense with the advantage of the support which a zone defense offers.

We believe that it is definitely best for our players to be assigned to a particular opponent—matching size, speed, and ability wherever possible. We do not encourage switching unless it becomes necessary because an offensive man is able to break free through a screen or other good maneuver.

Another advantage of the support man-to-man defense over the zone defense is that the man with the ball is played aggressively, thus restricting his opportunities for easy, open shots and eliminating that extra second the opponent might otherwise obtain in which to successfully gauge his shot.

Contrary to the belief of many coaches, we believe defensive rebounding is and should be much better in a support man-to-man than in a zone. The players in any man-to-man defense have the opportunity to *block out* (or to screen out) their respective opponents as a shot is being made. A zone makes it difficult to do this, since frequently there are two opponents charging a lone defensive player under the defensive board. Furthermore, the defensive zone players have the problem of looking for a man to block out, since no specific opponent has been assigned. Naturally, such a situation often leads to indecisiveness and uncoordinated play.

Outside players believe it easier to crash their offensive board against a zone than a man-to-man. They commonly contend the reason why good rebounding should supposedly result from a zone is that the big men are already set in defensive rebounding positions. Although this is undoubtedly true, it is not of very great importance because in our method match-ups are made according to size. We believe that smaller men can and should block out and rebound defensively against any opponent, from one shorter in height to one as much as four inches taller.

In addition to its possessing these important advantages over a zone defense, we feel our support man-to-man gives us a stronger defense against the lay-up or the close percentage shot. Certain areas which govern this principle are shown in Chart 94.

We refer to Area I as the scoring area and teach our players to make each pass and shot here as difficult as possible. First, we try to prevent an opponent from receiving a pass in this area (whether he be pivot man, scorer, or non-scorer). This is an important objective, but it does not necessarily prevent the score from being made; however, we find that there is less scoring than when we have failed to stress the point. A principal objective regarding Area I is to play aggressively up on the man with the ball. We tell our players they must play the man with the ball extremely tight or, as we say, "eat 'em up" in this Area.

Chart 94

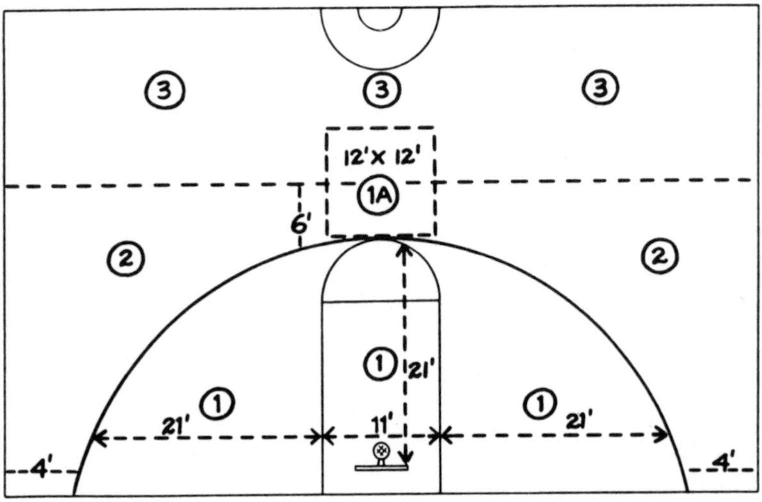

In Area I we are also "over the top" on all screens. That is, we allow no one between us and our opponent.

In Area II we continue to cover our respective men but not so aggressively. We have definite directions, depending upon our opponent's placement, in which we force a man with the ball in Area II to go. We slide through all screens in this area (between our defensive teammate and his opponent). A very essential point to understand in playing any defense is that you cannot prevent a team from taking shots during a game or hold them scoreless. From this philosophy, then, you must decide from what areas you want your opponents to shoot so that they will be less effective from a percentage standpoint. At South Carolina, we do not want our players to encourage opponents to shoot (except from Area III), but we tend to invite our opponents to shoot from Area II by defensive actions such as sliding through screens. We hope a shot will be attempted when our defender is close enough to bother the shooter and therefore decrease the percentage of shots turned into scores. In all my years of coaching I have seen few instances where a team or an individual on a team could win shooting from Area II, provided that the shooters were not given very much time actually to get off the shot. Of course, when a shot is taken from this area we must limit the opponent to that one shot by retrieving the rebound.

We have designated the 12′ by 12′ square at the top of the key Area A. In Area IA we play much the same as Area I. We do not want our opponents to handle the ball in this area without pressure. When an opponent has the ball in Area IA, he is in an ideal position to pass in all directions, thereby preventing us from executing the most important principle of forcing our opponents to play on only one side of the court or the other. We must not allow, then, a rapid swing or dribble of the ball whereby they may change sides quickly. If an opponent has the ball in Area IA, he is played most aggressively. Further, our defensive men who are guarding men in Area II move off their men more than usual, more or less inviting *the pass* from Area IA.

Since we cannot cover in practice sessions all possible offensive maneuvers and attacks against our support man-to-man defense, we attempt to teach the players certain principles which should remain constant no matter what the attack may be. Some of our defensive principles apply to any man-to-man defense, the support man-to-man included.

We usually begin by working on a good individual defensive technique for guarding a man with the ball. This, of course, is all important. Before beginning with the support defense, we spend a great deal of time with one-on-one and two-on-two situations where a defensive man cannot lean on support. If an individual can do a fairly good defensive job in these two situations, he should be an excellent operator in our support defense where we do not give him as many responsibilities.

The theory of support is based on forcing an opponent to do what you want him to do by your defensive position. We may say at the outset that position is all important. For instance, instead of playing a man "straight on," where he may drive right, drive left, or shoot over, we overplay him enough actually to rule out *one* of our opponent's electives. Thus, we force him to drive in the other direction if he is set to go on the dribble. By playing thus, the defensive man on the ball has actually lessened his responsibility. When he is forcing his opponent to drive one way, he is also expected to force him to pass the same way. It may appear that we are here setting a trap, so to speak, but what we actually want to do is limit the offense's attack and to prepare ourselves for the attack into which we are forcing them (see Charts 95 and 96).

As can be seen in Charts 95 and 96 the offense has made the pass we want (they also might have dribbled in the same direction). In either case we have them in Area II—just where we want them. Of course, there is usually movement by all offensive men when this pass is made, but we always begin explaining the defense by having the offensive men remain in their positions so that we can more readily instruct the defense players as to their respective positions.

In Chart 95 *B* was forcing 2 either to dribble or to pass to the sidelines by overplaying him. *A* was helping the decision by pressing 1 in Area II or Area IA. Should 1 move back into Area III, *A* then would allow the 2-to-1 pass. *D* allows and encourages the pass to 4 in Area II.

Chart 95

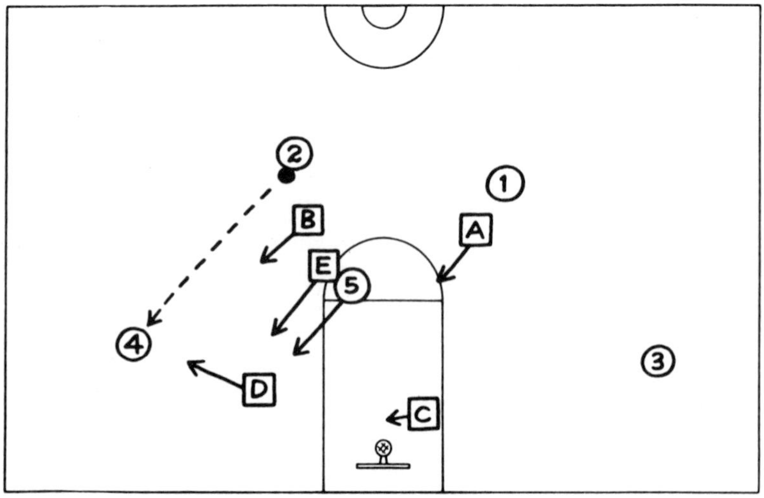

With the ball coming down either side and not in Area IA, *C* is given the opportunity to prepare for an attack on the right side of the court. He can set up an ideal position by straddling the lane in such a position that he can see both the ball and his man. Each of the five men is instructed to attempt to see both the ball and his man at all times. Should this be impossible, each of them must, at least, see his own man. *E*, the pivot defender, prepares for an attack to the right by moving to that side of his man (between his man and the ball). The importance of forcing the attack to the right as in Chart 95 is now obvious. Should the opponents be able to make a rapid pass to 1 in Area IA or 2, *E* and *C* would be in precarious positions, particularly *E*.

We declare our support men by two principles. First, if a man is two or three perimeter passes away from the ball (such as *C* in Chart 95 who is two passes away when 2 has the ball and three perimeter passes away when 4 has the ball), he may sag off his man many feet and be our *deep*, or *pivot*, support. We tell our players to make up most of this space on the pass that takes them from two passes away to one pass away. The *near* support man (*C* is deep support) is determined by the direction in which the man with the ball is being forced. In Chart 95, 2 is being forced toward 4. Therefore, *D* is our near support man.

We determine the direction in which we force by arbitrarily using the free throw line, extended all the way to the sideline. Outside of this area (where 2 is lined up), we force our opponents to the sideline. Inside this imaginary line we like to force our opponents to the middle

Chart 96

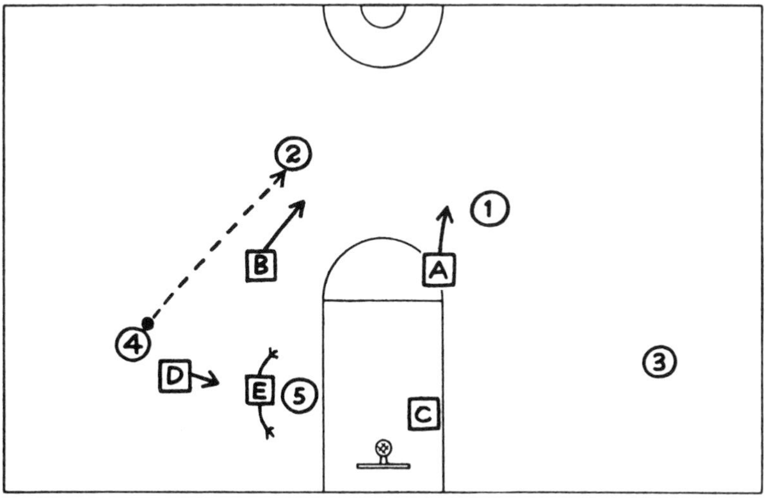

(away from the baseline). *Actually, we want to force the man with the ball to our nearest defensive "help" in Area II.* Extending the free-throw line in this manner provides a good guide and it is easy for our players to learn.

Continuing with the pass made in Chart 95, *B* follows the principle of "any man" defense by retreating in the direction in which the ball was thrown. If 2 elects to go away from the ball, *B* would be in no rush to go with him and should go no further than the lane if the ball remained with 4. Should 2 hold after passing to 4, *B* would then be the near support man with *C* continuing as deep support.

The pivot defense *E* must always attempt to be between his man 5 and the ball as long as 5 remains in this scoring area, Area I. We expect our players to prevent their men from receiving the ball in Area I by keeping their bodies facing the man and their heads turned so they can see both the ball and their man. For example, *E* in Chart 95 would place his left foot forward on a line between his man and the ball. His left arm would be extended out to deflect any pass to 5. Should 2 make a pass to 1 (we try to prevent this), *E* would have to continue around in front of 5 with his back to the ball until he was in position to turn his head and extend his right arm, since the ball would now be on his right.

In Chart 97, the principles continue to hold although a different offensive formation is met. First, *A* plays 1 aggressively to try to force him to pass or dribble out of Area IA. Both *B* and *C* are away from their men, thus encouraging a pass from 1. Here, the pass is going to 2, so *A* must retreat in that direction. *A* must also discourage a return pass to 1 in Area IA. *D* now becomes the near support man and, since the offense lacks a pivot man, we enjoy two deep support men—*C*, who is

Chart 97

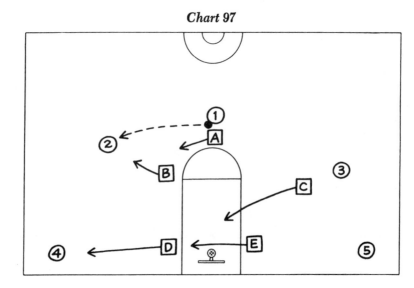

two passes away, and *E,* who is three perimeter passes away. Three perimeter passes are 2-1, 1-3, and 3-5.

Once an opponent uses up his dribble, our *near* support man should move out and press his man mildly, since he no longer has the responsibility to support on the drive. An important part of making this maneuver successful is a principle of any man-to-man defense—once your man uses up his dribble, move in aggressively. There are two objectives here: to be ready for the jump shot and to prevent a good release pass.

We have covered many of the defensive principles in our explanation of this support man-to-man. In our practices at South Carolina, we attempt to cover thoroughly those principles we believe to be imperative by defensive drills, drills, and drills. The support man-to-man defensive drills are used chiefly in teaching one principle at a time, gradually working into the game situations.

It may be necessary to explain exactly how we support before moving on to a few situations. If an opponent is not being contained, and is driving, our near support man waits until the last split second and then moves into the path of the driver with hands up. We intend this to be an aggressive, surprise move, to minimize the chance of a successful pass to the near support's offensive man. If a pass does get through, however, the near support man rushes back at his own man and should, in turn, receive help from some other teammate if it is needed. In supporting, we don't want our defensive players to reach for the dribbler, but actually to move in his path. Correct interpretation of the charge and block foul aids the effectiveness of this move.

We tell our boys that in Area I they must stop the open man and make the offensive man pass again, even if it means going out ten feet after an open man and leaving their men unguarded under the goal. We hope that by the time the pass under the goal can be attempted, support will have been received from a teammate.

As is readily seen, this support defense takes a great deal of time to perfect. A coach should spend an average of at least forty-five minutes a day on individual and team defense during the early stages of work on this defense. After spending a season in developing and perfecting the support defense, a coach will have a wonderful base upon which to build a pressing defense.

DISADVANTAGES OF THE MAN-TO-MAN DEFENSE

1. It requires a thorough understanding of defensive principles.

2. It is susceptible to screens, blocking, and other offensive tactics.

3. It permits fewer opportunities for interceptions because of the great amount of opponent-concentration required.

4. Players will commit more personal fouls.

5. It requires much movement and expenditure of energy.

6. Defensive and offensive situations are often missed because of opponent-concentration.

7. Offensive players have the advantage because of position (facing the basket) and can maneuver defensive players into blocks.

8. Opponents will capitalize upon team play if defensive players do not talk and cooperate to the fullest extent in sliding, going front, and switching.

9. Exceptional blocking-out ability is required on the part of all players to prevent easy follow-in scores by opponents.

10. There are fewer double-team opportunities.

8

the zone defenses

The straight man-to-man and the support man-to-man defenses are the basic defenses used at South Carolina University. We have, however, used the box-and-one and our point zones to good advantage against certain opponents, and in certain games we have used a sequence of shifting defenses, changing from the straight man-to-man (on a signal from the bench) to the box-and-one or to our point zone. At this point, it is perhaps important to point out that no defense is letter-perfect in its application or results. The coach who is seeking a defense that will successfully meet and check all offenses is doomed to a rude awakening. There is no *one* defense that can successfully meet all attacks.

The box-and-one zone defense

This is an unusual zone defense but can be highly effective against teams who concentrate on short shots for their scoring.

Defensive players *A, B, D,* and *E* form a box as shown in Chart 98. Behind the box, player *C* defends the under-basket area at all times. Chart 98 shows defensive player *A* forcing the offensive player 1 to the right. *A*'s box teammates are moving to the right to cover the overload on the right side of the court.

147

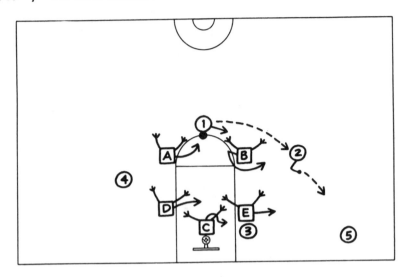

Chart 98

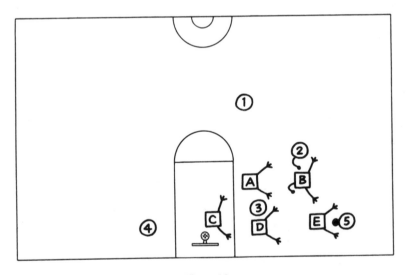

Chart 99

In Chart 99 offensive player 5 has the ball and the box has moved to the right side near the corner. Defensive player *E* has covered opponent 5 and his teammates *B*, *A*, and *D* make up the rest of the box while defensive player *C* is taking care of the underbasket area.

THE SOUTH CAROLINA UNIVERSITY
POINT ZONE DEFENSE

Combination zones are prevalent today. South Carolina University's point zone defense is a good example of such a combination zone. We combined some of the principles of the Two-One-Two zone with Clair Bee's original One-Three-One revolving zone and added our man-to-man support principles to make for a defensive set-up that has met with success.

In developing a combination zone, the coach employs special sagging and floating principles and attempts to direct the opponents' attack toward the side on which the team's strongest defensive players are stationed (since most teams are right-handed, the combination zone usually attempts to drive the opponents' attack to the defenders' right). Naturally, the team's best defensive players are placed on this side. Going further, use of a combination zone will permit the placement of one or two of the strongest and tallest rebounders in a position where their slides or moves will keep them in close proximity to the defensive board.

The point zone defense is predicated on basic principles which can be adapted by the players to all types of zone attacks. In this defense we are always playing the ball. We try to force the opponents to place an offensive man in each defensive man's zone. Obviously, this cannot be done if there is an exaggerated overload, say where an opponent lines up with five men on one-half of the court; however, most teams do not attack in this manner.

Our zone is unique in another respect. With the exception of the pivot man, we do not assign individuals to specific zones. With the necessity of our rotation, a man who starts out on the wing may end up "pointing" the ball in the corner on the opposite side of the court from that where he first lined up. Our zone cannot be considered strictly a One-Three-One, since it fluctuates with the type of attack the offense attempts; thus, it may look like a One-Three-One one time, a Two-One-Two on another occasion, and a Two-Three at another time.

As the basis for constructing the zone, the team forms on the point man (the offensive man with the ball). Theoretically, there should be three defensive men lined up between the ball and the goal—the point, the pivot, and the deep man. Flanking the pivot man are two wing men. Charts 100 and 101 show the initial set-up against a One-Three-One attack and a Two-One-Two attack.

The next important principle to remember in our zone is that each man changes his responsibility on each perimeter pass; each movement of the ball by the opponent necessitates a positive move by all five men playing the defense (point to wing; wing to point/or deep; deep to wing).

An exception to the principle of changing responsibility is when a perimeter pass (or a short dribble) goes no farther than six feet. Here, the man who was pointing the original man with the ball can go along with the dribbler or follow the short pass and point its receiver.

Chart 100

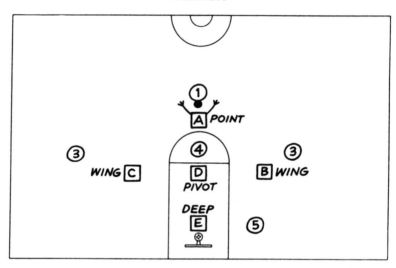

Chart 101

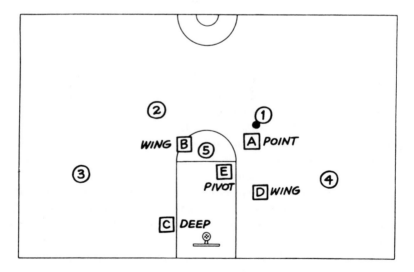

OBJECTIVES OF THE POINT ZONE DEFENSE

1. *To encourage hurried and long outside shots (outside the 21' scoring area).*

2. *To decrease fouling.*

3. *To provide a springboard for our fast break from a recovered rebound.*

Every man must know, and know well, the responsibility of each defensive position. We may often assign individuals to start on the point, the pivot, or the deep man; however, by the very nature of the game and the zone itself, there is no assurance that they will always be in such a controlled set-up. For example, after defending the fast break we are apt to have our smallest men starting in the deep positions (the pivot position included), and our pivot man may find himself filling in on the outside in the point or wing spots.

Responsibilities of each position

POINT MAN. The point man must try to force the ball in the same directions as our man-to-man defense principles dictate. This is generally to either sideline or to the nearest available support. (We found it very advantageous to pin the ball on the sidelines.) In the scoring area we play the point very tough and try to prevent a shot over us. The point man should be aggressive on the ball and play as though he was defending in a man-to-man situation. When the wing man relieves the point man of his point responsibility, the point man must retreat quickly to the vacant wing position.

If the ball should be returned in his direction, he again assumes the point. When a pass is made to the pivot, the point man's responsibility then becomes a quick, retreating slide to the front of the pivot man, a position from which he may return to point any opponent in his zone who may receive a return pass from the pivot.

WING MEN. The two wing men are the first line of support, and each of them has as his responsibility the duty to help defend against passes to the pivot as well as to protect against passes to the next receiver in his zone. Each wing man must be in a position to help support a teammate in meeting a one-on-one move by an opponent with the ball. If a pass is made to an opponent in his zone, the wing man becomes the point. If the pass goes around the perimeter in the opposite direction he then becomes the deep man. The wing's responsibility on a pass to the pivot is a quick, retreating slide toward the baseline to help support the pivot defense (pivot defense in this situation is actually the point).

DEEP MAN. The deep man has some of the most difficult and important responsibilities in this defense. He is the last line of defense. Theoretically, the deep man is on a line between the ball and the goal, but because of the possibility of a rapid swing, he must lean toward the man he may eventually have to point. If a pass is made to the pivot, the deep man must move to a position to jam any pass attempted toward the goal.

PIVOT MAN. The principal objectives of the pivot man are to block out successfully and to stop any scoring by a high or low post man. His most important slide in this position is the move down the lane when a pass or dribble is made to the baseline. If an opponent is on the lane (a low post), this slide should be in front of him, as shown in Chart 102.

When the opposing team uses a pivot attack, the offensive pivot player must be played according to the available scouting reports. Basically, our defensive pivot player should play behind his man, with an arm on the side on which the ball is being played, this to discourage a pass into the pivot. If the zone attack is a "shell" (having no stationary pivot), the defensive pivot should be alert for a "flash" pivot entering his area.

No two teams attack our point defense in the same manner. There has been similarity, however, in the varied offensive maneuvers with the principle of working the ball to the baseline. In the following situations, we shall cover the defense against these moves and a few more which might well be used against the point defense.

Chart 102

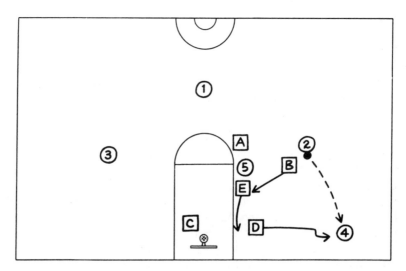

Although we follow closely our basic defensive principles no matter what the attack, we do make minor adjustments to stop any particular strong point the opponents might have developed to help them in attacking a zone. If a team plays a definite pattern against a zone, we usually cover this pattern in a practice just before coming up against them. It is in these practices that we make the necessary adjustments to fit the particular team and situation. Also, if a team has an excellent scorer, we may point extra tough on him or even use our point-and-one, which is the point defense with a major change—to play one player man-to-man against the high scorer with the other four men in the point zone with the pivot position out. This particular point-and-one defense (similar to the box-and-one or diamond-and-one) is shown in Charts 107 and 108.

In Chart 103, the offense is shown setting up two pivot men close to the lane. It may appear that 1 could easily throw a pass to 4 or 5. However, we have experimented with this particular pass and find it to be an unsuccessful gamble. If *C* and *B* were short players or if they were away from the lane, the pass might be successful, but this would not often be the case.

When 1 passes to 3, it is essential for *C* to move quickly and prevent a pass to 4 in close. *C* forces 3 in the direction of 1 (we tell our players to force the ball in the direction from which the pass came). *C* must bear in mind that he, as our point man, is defending 3 in a man-to-man defense, with good support from his teammates. *B* makes a fast move in

Chart 103

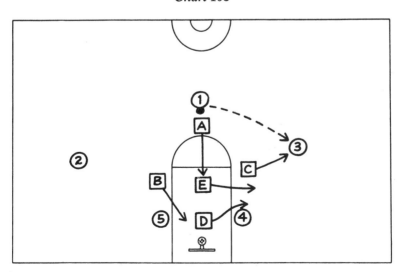

front of 5 and will block him out in the event 3 should shoot. *E* should attempt to be in line with the ball and goal, standing always ready for a flash pivot entering his area.

Continuing with the preceding Chart 103, let us start the ball with 3 (see Chart 104). We have 4 and 5 moving to the corner in this diagram, in a way in which some teams have elected to attack. *D* moves from just outside the lane to 4 as the pass is made to 4. *D*'s responsibility is to force 4 in toward *C*. *C*, in turn, should retreat quickly to jam up any high pivot action when 3 passes to 4. *E* must at the same time make his very important move to the approximate position where *D* was when 3 had the ball. *A* and *B* do not move on this pass (an exception to the principle of moving on each perimeter pass), since if they were to shift in accordance with our basic principle, *B* would go off the court to become a wing man and *A* would assume the deep position. Of course, this move with *A* and *B* would not be a good one at all, hence the reason for the exception to the principle in this particular situation.

In Chart 105 the offense has lined up with two men backcourt; our point zone now has the appearance of a Two-One-Two zone. Now, as 1 passes to 3 and cuts to the baseline to form a One-Three-One set-up, our point zone, in following the basic principles, now appears as a One-Three-One. On the pass to 3, our defensive men make the following moves: *A*, the point man, retreats to become a wing man, where he may help discourage a pass to the high post; *B*, who was a wing man when 1 had the ball, now moves back to become the deep man, since the pass

Chart 104

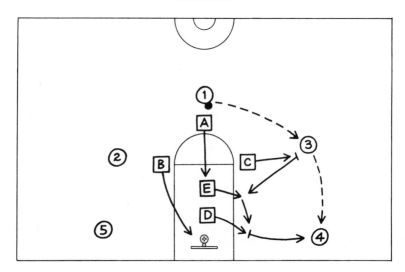

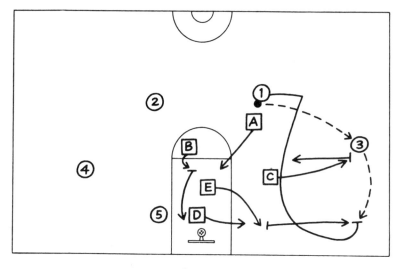

Chart 105

was made in the direction *away* from him, *C*, of course, becomes the point man and defends 3 as if we were playing a man-to-man; *D* makes an important move from one side of the lane to just outside the lane, and should have 1, who is cutting through, in sight at all times, for 1 is the man to point if and when he receives a pass from 3; *E* moves to a position in line with the ball and basket and looks for a flash pivot man.

POINT-AND-ONE DEFENSE

Whenever we decide to play our point-and-one defense, we are naturally sacrificing some of the strength of our zone in order to cover the dangerous opponent on a man-to-man basis. Our chief objective is to prevent him from receiving the ball. The other four men, who are setting up the point zone, use much the same principle that we use in the five-man point zone. We have now only a point man, two wing men, and a deep man. The latter is usually our center who has been transferred from his pivot position. Because of the hole left in the middle by this shift, our point-and-one becomes much more compact, allowing closer outside shots. This is the sacrifice we must make in order to stop our opponents' one good boy. One other factor which enters into the picture here is that it is most important for all four defensive men in the zone to go for the defensive rebound, as the opportunity to block out the offensive men is not as great here as in the five-man point zone.

In Chart 106 *A* is playing 1 man-to-man, preventing him from receiving the ball and making him reverse. *B* is the point man playing 2 as in a man-to-man defense. *C* and *D* are the wing men and are pinched in much more tightly than in the five-man zone. *E* is the deep man. Their moves can be readily seen from the diagram. The difference between this defense and the regular point zone is that when the pass to the corner is made, *D* must move across the lane to fill the spot which is

Chart 106

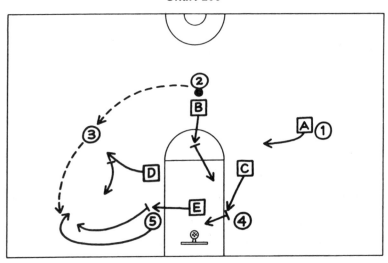

Chart 107

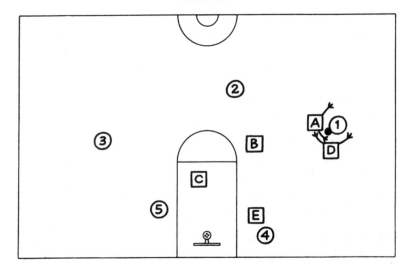

usually occupied by the pivot man. *B* therefore must move somewhat closer to the baseline than usual.

In Chart 107 1 is in possession of the ball. Although we do not wish for him to receive the ball, it cannot be absolutely prevented. *A* continues to play 1 aggressively, and *D*, who was a wing man, now becomes the point man on 1. Therefore, we have a double-team situation on the high scorer.

I would not recommend this point-and-one defense against a balanced scoring team. However, if one man is exceptional and you must stop him to win, I firmly believe this defense has a great deal of merit.

ADVANTAGES OF THE ZONE DEFENSE

1. The zone defense is fairly easy to teach and easy to understand.

2. The defensive arrangement may be coordinated with the planned offense.

3. The player arrangement permits freedom in attempting interceptions and the blocking of shots.

4. It reduces fouling as compared to the man-to-man defense.

5. The under-basket area is usually well protected and the recovery of the ball more certain than in the man-to-man defense.

6. Most zones are set up to take advantage of fast-break opportunities to a greater extent than the man-to-man defense.

7. The zone is especially effective in meeting screens and blocks.

8. Zones are effective on narrow courts because of the massing of the players in small areas.

9. The zone is effective against a dangerous pivot scorer.

10. It stops a driving and cutting attack.

11. A great many players prefer the zone to the man-to-man because they have a feeling of freedom and, to an extent, can forget opponent responsibility (assigned) and concentrate on the ball.

12. It is most effective against opponents who are poor ball handlers and weak outside shooters.

13. It can be used to good advantage against a weave, roll, or set offense.

14. *It can be used to good advantage as a surprise move or to give the defense a change of pace.*

15. *Zone defenses force opponents to make sharp and accurate passes.*

DISADVANTAGES OF THE ZONE DEFENSE

1. *A clever passing team will get a great number of short shots at the basket.*

2. *A well-poised team can tire out the zone players by movement of the ball and by cutting which keeps the ball hopping.*

3. *All zones are susceptible to good outside set shooting.*

4. *Overloading certain zone areas is fairly easy and places a heavy burden upon the outnumbered defensive players.*

5. *A team ahead can force the zone defense into man-to-man when they adopt the freeze near the end of the game.*

6. *Zone defensive players can be faked out of position and are easy to go around with or without the ball.*

7. *An offensive player working on the baseline can easily get the inside position for easy tap-in and follow-in shots.*

8. *Use of the zone defense without proper man-to-man training can handicap a high school player when he goes to college.*

9. *Blocking tactics can be employed to good advantage to permit open shots on the side opposite the overloaded areas.*

10. *Tall, slower players can operate against the zone defense to better advantage than the man-to-man defense.*

9

combination defenses

Combination defenses are so complex and numerous that it would require an entire text to outline and describe their applications. For our purposes at South Carolina University we have found the screen-switch, the one-man zone, and the Box-and-One defense sufficient to take care of unusual problems. For clarification, our Box and One places the box in front of the basket and assigns one of our better defensive players to guard the opponents' key player or high-scoring star wherever he may go on a man-to-man basis.

THE SCREEN-SWITCH DEFENSE

The screen-switch defense combines zone and man-to-man defense principles. It masses its players zone-fashion in front of the basket and also utilizes the individual guarding principles of the man-to-man defense.

The chief advantages of the screen-switch defense are its effectiveness against screening and blocking, the amount of footwork it saves over the assigned man-to-man defense, its adaptation in the use of the full-court press, and its massing of players near the basket for rebound protection.

The major disadvantages of the screen-switch defense are that it does not permit consistent assignment of players to particular opponents and it is difficult to teach.

In the screen-switch defense, the defensive players switch every time an inside or back screen is used by the opponents. When an outside screen or a diagonal cut is made by an opponent, there is no switch unless a post or pivot block is encountered. Then, the teammate guarding the post or pivot player switches and the defensive roll is used by the player guarding the cutter to get position on the post or pivot player.

When the screen-switch defense is used expertly it is difficult to crack. It permits the extensive use of sagging and floating. Although the constant switching may seem to make the matching of men unimportant, this is not so. Players are matched as usual at the first center jump and matching is continued in all held-ball situations, in taking positions on the lane in free-throw formations, in the defensive out-of-bounds formations, and when the opponents advance upcourt to set up their attack. Charts 108 and 109 illustrate the use of this excellent defense.

In Chart 108 offensive player 1 passes the ball to his teammate 2 and executes an inside screen. Defensive player A follows his opponent 1 until the screen is made and then shifts to guard player 2. Defensive player B shifts to guard opponent 1 as soon as the screen is made.

Offensive player 5 drives his opponent E into the block set by offensive player 3 beside the lane. Defensive player E follows 5 until

Chart 108

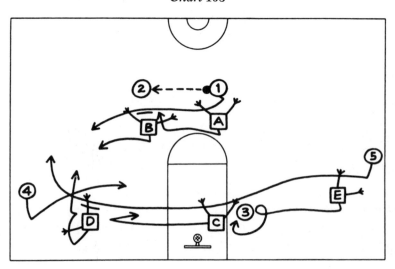

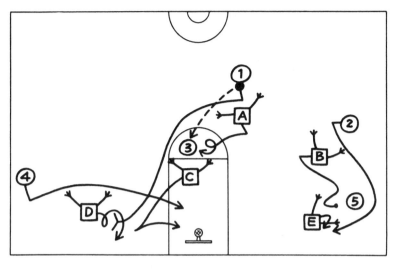

Chart 109

his teammate *C* calls the switch. Then defensive player *E* shifts to guard opponent 3 by using the defensive roll. Defensive player *C* shifts to opponent 5 and follows him to the other side of the court. When opponent 5 screens against defensive player *D*, *C* shifts to opponent 4 and *D* shifts to cover opponent 5.

It is well known that best offense against the switch-defense is the use of change-of-direction plays in the back court and post-and-pivot plays in the front court. Chart 109 shows the diagonal attack and the resulting shifts by the screen-switch players. Player 1 (with the ball) fakes to his left and passes the ball to the post player 3. Player 1 cuts through and past his teammate 3 on the post. Defensive player *A* shifts to guard opponent 3 by use of the defensive roll. Defensive player *C* shifts to the cutter 1.

When the cutter 1 sets a block behind defensive *B*, defensive player *C* will pick up offensive player 4 when he drives toward the basket. Defensive player *D* will use the defensive roll to get into position to guard the offensive blocker 1. On the weak side of the court, defensive player *B* will shift to guard opponent 5 and defensive player *E* will shift to take offensive player 2.

One-man zone defense

The one-man zone defense can be used efficiently against a strong double-post or double-pivot attack. Many strong teams have a low-scoring player on the team for defensive balance. If the roamer can be assigned to guard this opponent, his value to the defense will be increased. The roamer must fake to cover his low-scoring opponent when a scoring play seems unlikely and should leave him to play in front of a post or pivot player when these dangerous players get into position. The roamer is given unlimited freedom and is on his own at all times.

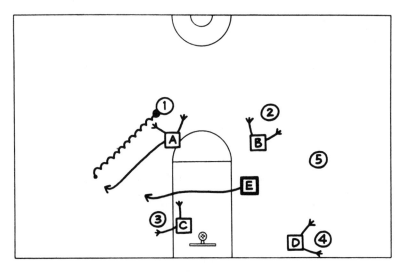

Chart 110

Chart 110 illustrates the one-man zone defense. Defensive player *E* is the roamer applying zone tactics while his teammates use man-to-man principles. Here offensive player 1 dribbles toward the sideline guarded by his assigned opponent *A*. Defensive player *E* (the roamer) has apparently been playing opponent 5. However, player *E* has now cut to a position between the dribbler and the opponents' pivot man 3 to discourage a pass or possibly to make an interception.

Box and One

The use of a roamer who may be assigned to guard (dog) the opponents' star scorer or ball-handler is fairly common. It has been used in combination with the zone defense in several forms. At South Carolina University we employ a box formation immediately in front of the basket and assign our best defensive player to dog the important opponent.

The roamer is permitted unlimited freedom. He may assist in the general defense and still stick with the key player, help double-team when the opportunity presents itself, and try to steal the ball at all times. Frequently he breaks all alone for his basket when the opponents take a shot. All of these possibilities add up to a job that requires a strong, "40-minute player" who loves action.

Chart 111

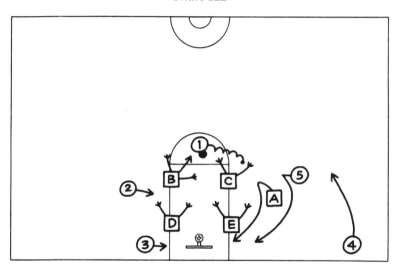

Chart 112

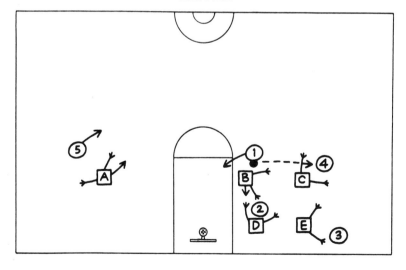

In Chart 111 offensive player 5 is the high-scoring opponent and is being guarded by the roamer who will dog him wherever he may go. Defensive players *B, C, D,* and *E* have formed a box in front of the basket and employ zone tactics against the general attack. Here, attacking player 1 is dribbling toward the side of the court and will be picked up by defensive player *C* while he is in that zone area. Offensive player 5 is cutting toward the basket guarded by *A.*

In Chart 112 defensive player *A* (the roamer) is dogging his opponent wherever he goes. Defensive players *B, C, D,* and *E* are setting up a box zone on the right side of the court.

In Chart 113 player *A* continues to dog his assigned star opponent. Offensive player 4 passes the ball to 5 who is closely guarded by the roamer *A.* Defensive players *B, C, D,* and *E* have now set up the box zone between the ball and the basket to add to offensive player 5's difficulties in breaking loose for a score.

Chart 113

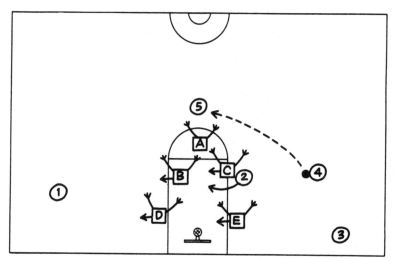

10

defensive game situations

PLAYING THE LANE

The inside defensive positions on the lane should be occupied by the tallest and strongest rebounders on the squad. If the free throw is made, one of the rebounders should catch the ball before it hits the floor and pass it to the other who has stepped out of bounds. These two players and an alternate should employ simple signals to designate which rebounder will get the ball and which will move to the out-of-bounds position.

Many teams employ the fast break from defensive free-throw situations whether the attempt is successful or not. Speed is important and the ball should be put in play as quickly as possible. When the basket is missed, the rebounder should leap as high as possible and tap the ball to a teammate in the corner. Here, the corner players should warn the rebounders if opponents move toward them to apply the press or to attempt to intercept the ball. In this case, of course, the rebounders will eliminate the tap and catch the ball.

The defenders (the rebounders and the teammate guarding the opponent attempting the free throw) will first concern themselves with blocking the offensive players away from the board; then they will concentrate upon recovering the ball. The player guarding the shooter must step into the lane as soon as the ball touches the backboard or the rim of the basket. His primary objective is to get between the shooter and the basket and then retrieve the ball if it rebounds in his direction.

Many important tap-in shots are scored because the two defensive players next to the basket do not block their dangerous opponents away from the ball. It is equally dangerous for them to allow their opponents to force them under the basket where they can't possibly recover the ball.

Stepping directly forward into the lane and under the basket is just as foolish, since the defensive player is then too far under the basket and the opponent merely moves along the line and into the inside position and taps the ball back up for a possible score.

Chart 114

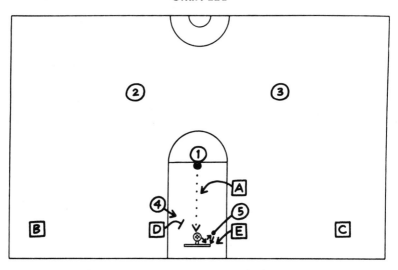

Chart 114 shows defensive player *D*, on the left side of the lane, blocking his opponent 4 away from the possible rebound. Defensive player *E*, on the right side of the lane, has stepped straight forward under the basket permitting his opponent, player 5, to step directly forward and tap the ball back up on the board. Defensive player *A* has stepped correctly into the lane and is blocking the shooter from advancing up the lane to follow-in the shot.

Chart 115 illustrates the common rebound principle of tapping an unsuccessful free-throw rebound to a teammate on the side of the court or in the corner. Defensive player *E* blocked opponent 5 away from the board and leaped high in the air to tap the ball over to teammate *C*. Player *A* blocked opponent 1 from the basket and when he saw re-

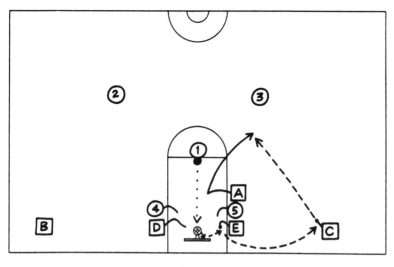

Chart 115

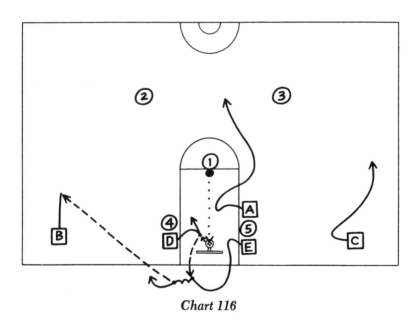

Chart 116

bounder E tap the ball, broke upcourt for the fast break. On the other side of the lane, defensive player D blocked opponent 4 away from the board.

In Chart 116 defensive player D has signalled teammate rebounder E to move out of bounds after blocking his opponent to make the throw-in. Naturally, defensive rebounder E will block opponent 5 away from the board until he is sure teammate D will get the ball as it comes through the net. Time is of the essence here, but defensive E must be sure to block his opponent away from the basket unless the ball comes cleanly through the basket. Defensive player A has blocked the shooter away from the board; as soon as he sees the shot is good he will start the fast-break drive.

JUMP-BALL AND OUT-OF-BOUNDS PLAYS

Defense against auxiliary plays, the freeze, and the stall attack is important because a lessening of vigilance or a mistake at a critical time may result in loss of the game. Zone tactics are unquestionably superior to man-to-man principles in meeting the auxiliary plays, while the press and an aggressive screen-switch defense are more effective than zone applications when meeting the freeze and the stall. Meeting the freeze and the stall will be discussed in the next chapter.

The advantage of zone tactics over the man-to-man defense against out-of-bounds situations lies in the fact that no specific opponent must be guarded, and the nearest defensive player may guard the out-of-bounds or the under-basket opponent.

Defensive formations for the center-tap and held-ball situations are fairly uniform, but defensive measures for out-of-bounds plays take a number of forms and both man-to-man and zone defenses are applied.

When opponents have a lead and time is running out, it is necessary to do something to get the ball. The same urgency is present when the opponents have a lead and are using an offensive stall to hold on to the ball until a sure shot can be attempted.

Jump-ball defense

When the opponents consistently control the tap, an attempt must be made to steal the ball. Such attempts, however, should not be made at the expense of defensive balance. In Charts 117 through 123 defensive balance is given first consideration.

In Chart 117 player 1 controls the tap. Defensive balance permits only defensive players B and C opportunity to steal the ball. Players B and C wait until opponent 1 taps the ball and then break as shown. If unsuccessful in obtaining the ball, they fall back as shown to pick up their opponents 2 and 3.

In Chart 118 a revolving method is used to attempt to intercept the ball. Player 1 controls the tap. In order to provide defensive balance, player E drops back as shown for defense, and his teammates B, C, and D rotate in counterclockwise fashion. In this case, opponent 1 taps the ball toward his teammate 3. Player *B* cuts outside the circle until the ball is tapped and then drives in front of opponent 3 to intercept the ball.

Chart 117

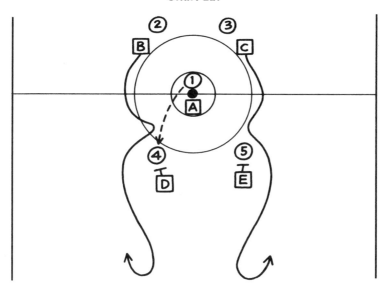

Chart 118

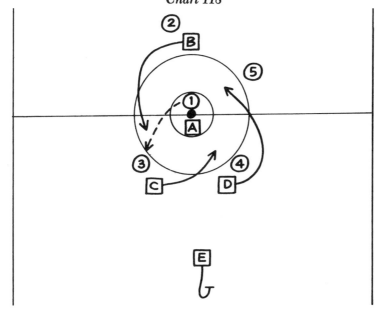

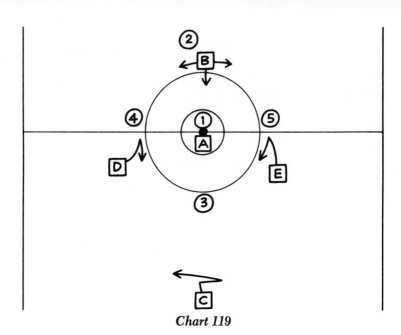

Chart 119

Chart 120

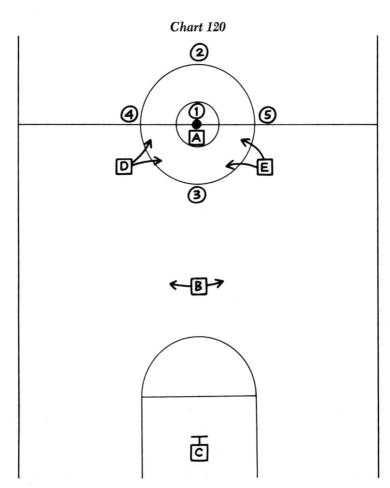

Chart 119 shows a zone defense set up for the center jump. It can be used with the Two-Three zone formation or with the Three-Two as well as the Two-One-Two zone defense.

The zone center-jump formation in Chart 120 can be used by practically any zone. The players are set so that they can drop straight back into a Three-Two, One-Three-One, Two-One-Two, or a Two-Three zone defense.

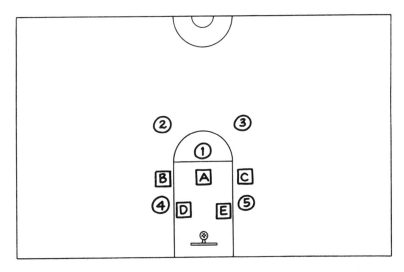

Chart 121

Chart 122

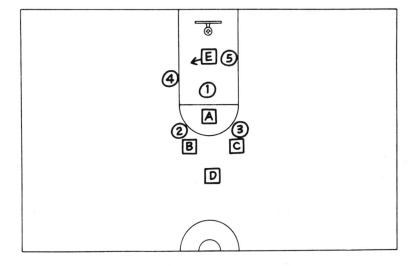

Chart 121 shows a defensive position assumed in opponents' front court when they have a tap advantage. Here, defensive players B and C have dropped back to discourage opponent 1 from making a front tap. They are in a good position to play their opponents 2 and 3 or get the ball.

Chart 122 shows a defensive position assumed in one's own front court when expecting to lose the tap. Player D is the defensive man. Teammates B, C, and E try to anticipate the tap but B and C must be ready to drop back for defensive balance.

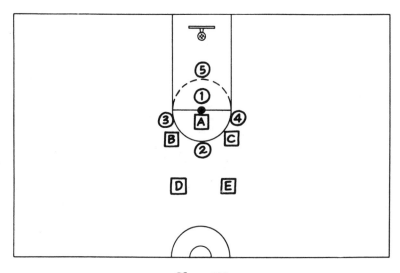

Chart 123

Chart 123 shows a front-court zone jump-ball formation. Here, the Three-Two zone defense formation is already set up. Naturally it is a defensive alignment, but it offers competition for any tap except a back tap by opponent 1.

Checking out-of-bounds plays

In attacking the man-to-man defense, opponents attempt to free a teammate under the basket for an easy shot through the use of screens, posts, and blocks. We have found it necessary to use the switch in our man-to-man defensing against under-basket out-of-bounds plays. When we are using a zone defense (Two-One-Two) we have little trouble in guarding the under-basket area but find it difficult to check the 18- and

20-foot shots. Charts 125 through 128 show how we attempt to meet the out-of-bounds plays with the zone and the man-to-man defense.

In Chart 124 the Two-One-Two zone is set up to protect the under-basket area. The zone players will hold the integrity of the zone but will cover the receiver of the first pass quickly. All are prepared to move in the directions shown by the arrows.

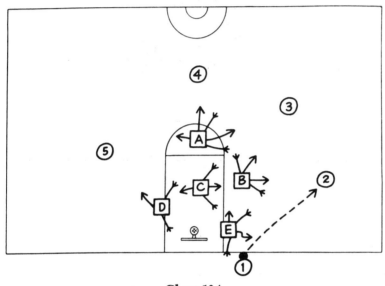

Chart 124

Chart 125 shows a common type of out-of-bounds formation which is designed to trap offensive player 2's opponent in the blocks set by his teammates 3, 4, and 5. Opponent 2's guard is defensive player *B*. He is prepared to pick up 2 if he cuts as shown. If 2 cuts to the other side, defensive player *E* will switch to him; *B*, *C*, and *D* will slide to the right and cover 3, 4, and 5 respectively.

If the ball is thrown to opponent 2 in the outer half of the free-throw area, player *B* will chase him and opponents 3, 4, and 5 will be covered by defensive players *C*, *D*, and *E*. Defensive player *B* can play opposite 2 in the outer half of the free-throw circle but there is great danger of opponent 2's driving him into the block set by teammates 3, 4, and 5. A switch would then be necessary, and the opponent into whom *B* is driven would be on the inside position and could cut to the basket for an easy shot. We prefer to force the long outside pass.

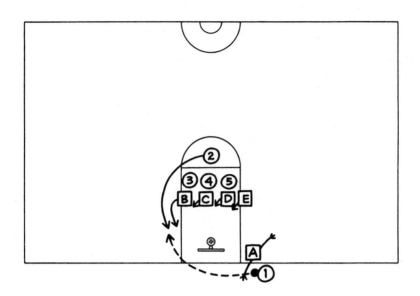

Chart 125

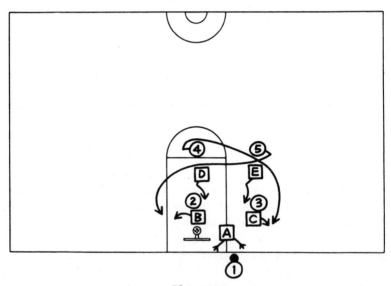

Chart 126

Chart 126 shows a common box type of out-of-bounds play. In this setup a switch is necessary by defensive players *B, C, D,* and *E. B,* and *C* must take the cutters (opponents 4 and 5); *D* and *E* must drive to the inside of the lane to switch to opponents 2 and 3.

A zone alignment (Two-One-Two; Three-Two; Two-Three) is

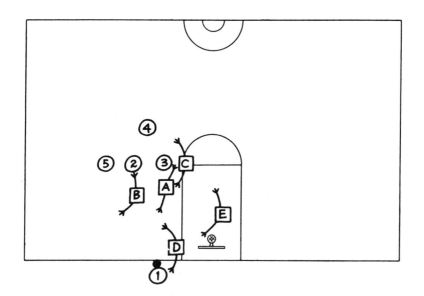

Chart 127

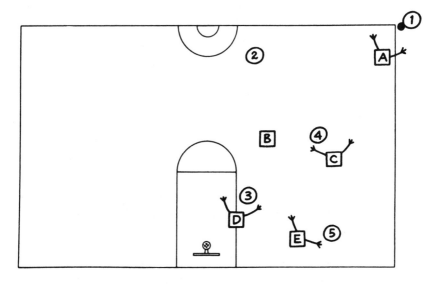

Chart 128

shown in Chart 127. This type of setup counters cutting and screening out-of-bounds plays. About the only safe pass-in is to offensive player 4 in the backcourt. Note that the defensive players are facing sideways so that they can watch the ball and the opponents at the same time.

In Chart 128 the zone formation is set up to a center line (ten-second line) out-of-bounds play by opponents. The formation shown is in a One-Two-Two alignment but can be shifted quickly into any zone.

MEETING THE FREEZE AND THE STALL

The freeze

When your team is behind in the score and the opponents initiate a freeze, your players must know exactly what they must do in their attempts to get the ball. Some opponents will start their freeze when they have but a one-point lead and with as much as five minutes left to play. This is unusual, however, and most teams will employ some form of the stall or possession offense at this stage of the game.

The actual freeze is usually employed when two minutes or less remain to be played and the opponents want to maintain their lead and retain possession of the ball till the game ends.

Should the opponents employ a one-man freeze through the use of the dribble, your most agile guard (usually a backcourt quarterback) must be assigned to play him aggressively wherever he may go without committing a foul. His teammates must be prepared to pick up the dribbler if he succeeds in getting loose.

If the opponents use some sort of a weave, the screen-switch should be used every time there is a crossing of players. Should the opponents avoid crossing and the attending double-teaming opportunities, every player must play his opponent on a man-to-man basis and stick with him. There is no easy solution here—hours of practice time must be spent in teaching your players to guard an opponent so closely that he cannot get free to receive or pass the ball.

If close guarding is not proving successful, your players must be prepared to make interception and double-teaming attempts. Naturally, interception attempts are most successful against cross-court passes, and double-teaming succeeds best when applied in the corners (front- and backcourt corners).

The coach must act to help his team by substituting his fleetest players when his team is behind and the clock is running out. Size is no longer an important factor; speed is of the essence, and the coach should beat the opponents to the punch by applying the press before they can employ the freeze.

Should one of your players make an interception and advance the ball to the frontcourt, he and his teammates must be prepared to maintain the press following a successful or unsuccessful try for a score.

Further, greater chances may be taken in the frontcourt because of the distance from the opponents' basket.

The stall

Some teams initiate a stall attack when they are as much as ten points ahead of a dangerous opponent and when there is as much time as seven or eight minutes left to play. Many coaches believe that this is folly and that a team should never change its offense or pace when it is winning. The wisdom of the change from a successful attack to a stall offense is certainly debatable, but conditions govern many such decisions and it is just one more of the game problems facing the coach.

Quite a few teams hold their stall attack in abeyance until there is only a short time left in the game. An important phase of the stall at any time is the ability of the offensive players to conceal the fact that they are employing a stall attack.

No matter what the offensive strategy, all teams should be prepared to meet the stall when they are behind in the score. Conceding possession of the ball to opponents when they are ahead is as bad as conceding a basket to a player who makes an interception and dribbles toward his team's basket. A good defensive team concedes nothing and puts out until the last second and the last basket.

Naturally, if the defensive team does not make an attempt to get the ball, the opponents may change their tactics and apply the freeze.

Chart 129

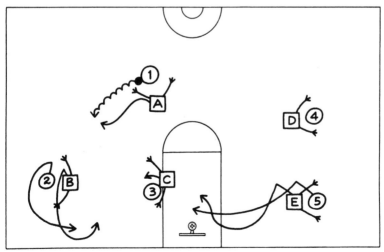

It is best to play a tight defense and make an effort to get the ball under any circumstances.

When the stall is being used, the defense must keep in mind that the opponents will try to score to keep the defensive team defense-minded.

Chart 129 shows a way of meeting the stall. Defensive player *A* is playing his opponent 1 tightly to prevent him from making a good pass. With the exception of *A*, the other defensive players are purposefully violating the man-to-man in-line principle so that they may be in good positions to attempt interceptions. Defensive players *B*, *D*, and *E* must be careful not to let opponents 2, 4, or 5 use a change-up to cut toward the basket. Here, offensive players 2 and 5 are attempting the change-up, but defensive players *B* and *E* have anticipated the move and have covered them closely.

11

the press
and its variations

INTRODUCTION

At South Carolina University the full-court press is considered second in importance only to our basic man-to-man defense and to our point zone. We use the full-court press as a strategy move if we feel that it may upset our opponents, and we also use it as a full-game defense against certain opponents.

Against a particular opponent, the press may cause the players to use up valuable time-outs early in the game; perhaps it will force them to remove their big man from the game; it may affect the play of their big man or men even though they are left in the game; and it may give us a psychological edge.

In setting up our full-court press, each player picks up and sticks with his assigned opponent. No switching is permitted in the opponents' backcourt. Following a score, the player assigned to guard the opponent who takes the ball out of bounds will drop away from him and attempt to double-team and steal the ball or tie it up for a jump ball. This double-teaming is applied to the opponents' best dribbler or passer if possible.

The single-man press is often used to surprise opponents; frequently two or three of our best chasers may put on a press. When we apply our half-court press, the opponents are met at the center line and played tightly in an attempt to force them into errors or violations. Dribblers are forced to the sidelines and weak ball handlers are double-teamed at every opportunity.

The full-court press demands that the players be in tip-top condition and be equipped with some form of an organized attack. We spend a lot of time in perfecting the press and have found that best results are obtained through the use of four small players plus a big man who is exceptionally fast.

The press is applied following a score from the field, after a successful or unsuccessful free throw, following a violation or an interception. Our players are expected to pick up their opponents immediately and stick with them. Naturally, there will be mistakes, and opponents will often get free and break into their frontcourt. This is expected; we simply accept it as one of the breaks of the game and hurry back to set up our regular defense.

It is more important that each player develop the ability to know where his assigned opponent is at all times. A good way to achieve this ability is to give the pressing team the ball and require each player to pick up his particular opponent as soon as the ball is lost. Another good practice is one-on-one defensive play in which the pressing player attempts to force his opponent (with the ball) toward the sideline. Our players are taught to attempt to steal the ball by slapping *up* at it, but they are not permitted to sacrifice a good guarding position in order to attempt a steal.

THE FULL-COURT PRESS

Apply the press

"When your side loses the ball, get your man immediately and stick to him like glue." Dr. James A. Naismith, the inventor of basketball, wrote that in his original rules of the game and it just about tells the story with respect to the use of the press.

There are many ways to employ this important team asset. Some teams use the full-court press during the entire game. Others apply it intermittently as a surprise element.

There are many variations of the full-court press. These include the semi-court press (meeting opponents at the ten-second line and playing them tightly to force them into errors), the surprise press (use of double-teaming when an opponent can be attacked in the double-teaming areas), and various types of the zone press.

In the man-to-man defense some teams play without the use of the switch; many switch every time the ball is exchanged; others switch every time opponents cross.

WHEN TO USE THE PRESS

1. When we want to surprise a team and attempt to upset their poise. We hurry them and attempt to force bad passes, make them travel with the ball or fumble it.

Chart 130

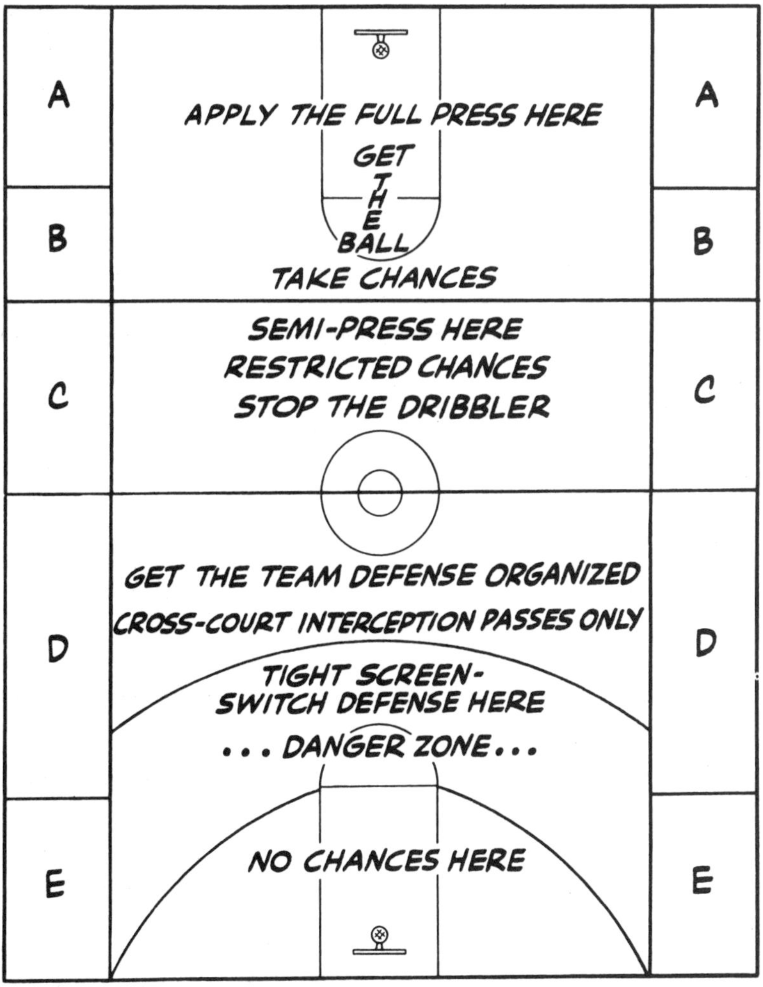

A	APPLY THE FULL PRESS HERE	A
	GET T H E	
B	BALL TAKE CHANCES	B
C	SEMI-PRESS HERE RESTRICTED CHANCES STOP THE DRIBBLER	C
D	GET THE TEAM DEFENSE ORGANIZED CROSS-COURT INTERCEPTION PASSES ONLY TIGHT SCREEN- SWITCH DEFENSE HERE ... DANGER ZONE ...	D
E	NO CHANCES HERE	E

2. *When we face opponents who are bigger and perhaps slower and who feature the slow advance and a possession offensive style.*

3. *When we are behind in the score near the end of the game and must have the ball.*

The use of the full-court press means playing opponents all over the court. We attempt to play each opponent tightly and hope to make it difficult for him to receive or pass the ball.

When an opponent takes the ball out-of-bounds on the baseline, we usually give him complete freedom and concentrate on covering all possible receivers. We station the player assigned to the out-of-bounds opponent midway between the two downcourt opponents. Other opponents are played closely and aggressively. The free man in the press is expected to attempt to double-team the first receiver. If this is impossible, he is expected to pick up his out-of-bounds opponent and "stick to him like glue."

Defense positioning is vital. We expect each of our players to play no more than one step away from his opponent and on an inside position. Every player must position himself so he will be able to see his opponent and the ball at all times. The switch is imperative. However, it must not be made unless the opponents actually cross and are so close together that there is no possibility of a change of direction. This means that there will be a slight delay in picking up opponents on the switch, but the inside position permits this slight slacking off.

All players must be aggressive without fouling and be interception and double-team minded. When an opponent has the ball, he must be played tightly with hands moving up and down and from side to side to discourage a pass. Other opponents may be given a little room so that a sudden dash will not leave the defensive player behind.

The court is divided into areas as shown in Chart 130.

Area A. Always attempt to double-team an opponent who has the ball here.

Area B. Attempt double-teaming only when teammate has the opponent well guarded

Area C. No double-teaming unless teammate has forced opponent to pivot away until his back is to his own basket.

Area D. Same principle as used in Area C.

Area E. Always attempt to double-team an opponent who has the ball here.

VARIATIONS OF THE PRESS

Single-man press

The single-man press is a surprise move that often results in a quick score. The ability of the defensive man to play dummy often throws the man with the ball off guard. Then, a sudden whirl and a fast advance by the defensive player may catch the dribbler asleep and cause him to make a violation. Frequently, the move may result in a steal.

Chart 131 shows a single-man press. Defensive player B has played dummy and started upcourt with his back to the receiver of the pass from out-of-bounds (2). B whirls suddenly and presses opponent 2, trying to force him toward the sideline or to steal the ball.

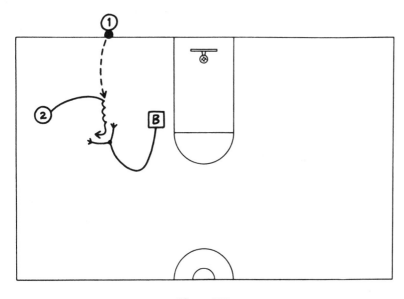

Chart 131

The two-man press

Two clever, fleet-footed backcourt players can often apply the two-man press with good success. Here, again, the chief element of success lies in surprise and a sudden attack. The surprise is necessary in order to disguise the intention to press so that other teammates will not come to the assistance of the two opponents.

Chart 132 shows a two-man press. Here, defensive player A plays dummy and then charges the dribbler (opponent 2) and forces him toward the sideline. Immediately thereafter, defensive teammate *B* dashes back and covers opponent 1.

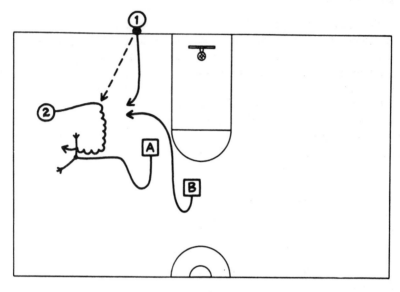

Chart 132

Three-quarter press

The three-quarter press is applied when the opponents' big men are in the habit of advancing rapidly to their frontcourt leaving two backcourt teammates to advance the ball. The two defensive chasers meet these players midway between the free-throw circle and the ten-second line.

The defensive player opposing the man with the ball tries to force him toward the sideline and to turn his back to the frontcourt. When this occurs, the other chaser is expected to double-team the man with the ball. Whenever the double-teaming is attempted, one of the defensive players guarding the opponents who have advanced to the front-court will dash back to guard the uncovered player in the opponents' backcourt. The remaining defensive players will move to zone positions where they may be able to cover the players most likely to receive a possible pass.

Chart 133 shows a three-quarter press. Defensive players *A* and *B* have advanced to meet opponents 1 and 2. Defensive player *A* has forced the dribbler 1 toward the left sideline and offensive player 1 has turned toward the backcourt. When this occurs, defensive player *B*

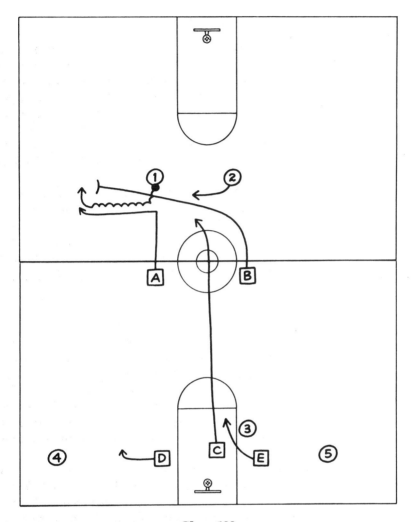

Chart 133

leaves offensive 2 and attempts to double-team the dribbler. Defensive player *C* moves forward to guard offensive 2; defensive players *D* and *E* move to the positions shown. If offensive player 1 succeeds in passing the ball forward to one of his teammates in the front court, defensive player *C* must retreat quickly and teammate *B* must return to guard opponent 2.

When there is no double-teaming opportunity, the defensive players will stick tightly to their opponents and hope for a bad pass and a chance to make an interception.

Semi-press

Many teams use a sort of press which, for lack of a better term, may be called a semi-press. The decision to apply this press rests solely with any defensive player and is usually applied in the defensive half of the court. Its application depends upon the mistakes of individual opponents. Opportune times for its application include: when an opponent fumbles the ball and then recovers it; following a dribble when the dribbler stops (he's dead!) and does not immediately pass the ball; or when an attacking opponent turns, faces, or pivots so that his back is toward his basket.

The semi-press is a spontaneous and surprise maneuver and may be initiated by any defensive player who sees an opportunity to take advantage of an opponent's mistake or uncertainty. As soon as a defensive player attacks his opponent in one of the above situations, his teammates should immediately press their respective opponents, anticipating a bad pass or an opportunity to double-team the man with the ball.

The zone press

We have used the Two-One-Two zone press at times but prefer to concentrate on the man-to-man press. When we are employing the Two-One-Two zone as the game defense, we frequently use the same formation in applying the press. The two frontcourt chasers bear the brunt of this zone press; our most agile players are assigned the job. The middle man ranks next in agility requirements so the third best press player should have the job. The two rear players are the two best rebounders (the big men).

Chart 134 illustrates the zone-press lanes and the positions and duties of the zone players. Defensive zone-press players A and D are responsible for the left sideline lane from baseline to baseline. Defensive zone-press players B and E are responsible for the right sideline lane from baseline to baseline. Defensive zone-press player C is responsible for the middle lane from baseline to baseline.

In Chart 134 the slides shown are appropriate when the ball is in the position shown. Player 1 has the ball out-of-bounds. Defensive player A plays opponent 2 closely as shown. Defensive player B has left his lane because it was empty and has cut across into the middle lane to cover opponent 3. Defensive zone-press player C has also left his lane because 3 has left it (covered by B) and now covers opponent 4. Downcourt, player D (in his lane) has advanced because opponent 5 is advancing (fishhooking) and because it is empty. Defensive player E has left his lane to cover opponent 5.

Defensive players *D* and *E* are slow to commit themselves on any play since they are responsible for the entire defensive area under the opponents' basket. They must watch the middle lane when teammate *C* plays in an advanced position. No matter what the play, a defensive player does not leave his lane when it is occupied unless a teammate is covering an opponent for him as in the case of *C* and *B* here.

Chart 134

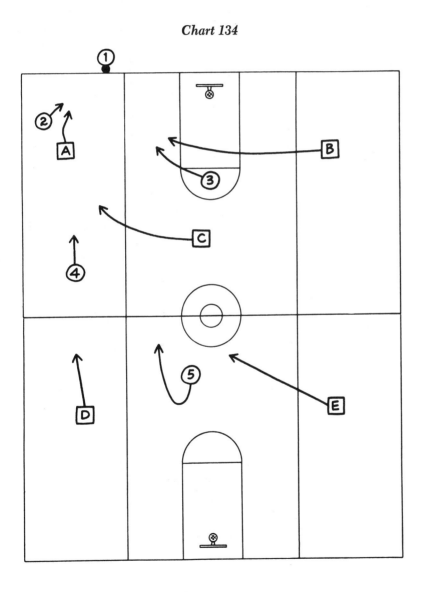

The South Carolina combination press

We alternate the man-to-man and the Two-One-Two zone (See Chart 135) to establish our combination (pressure) defense. From experience we have found that it is comparatively easy to shift from a man-to-man full-court press into a Two-One-Two zone press at three-quarter or half-court.

In our initial man-to-man move we do not always oppose the out-of-bounds player. When we fake this coverage, it means we are prepared to double-team the opponent to whom the pass from out-of-bounds is made. Frequently, we pass up the trap on the first receiver and concentrate on the second receiver. The second pass is usually made

Chart 135

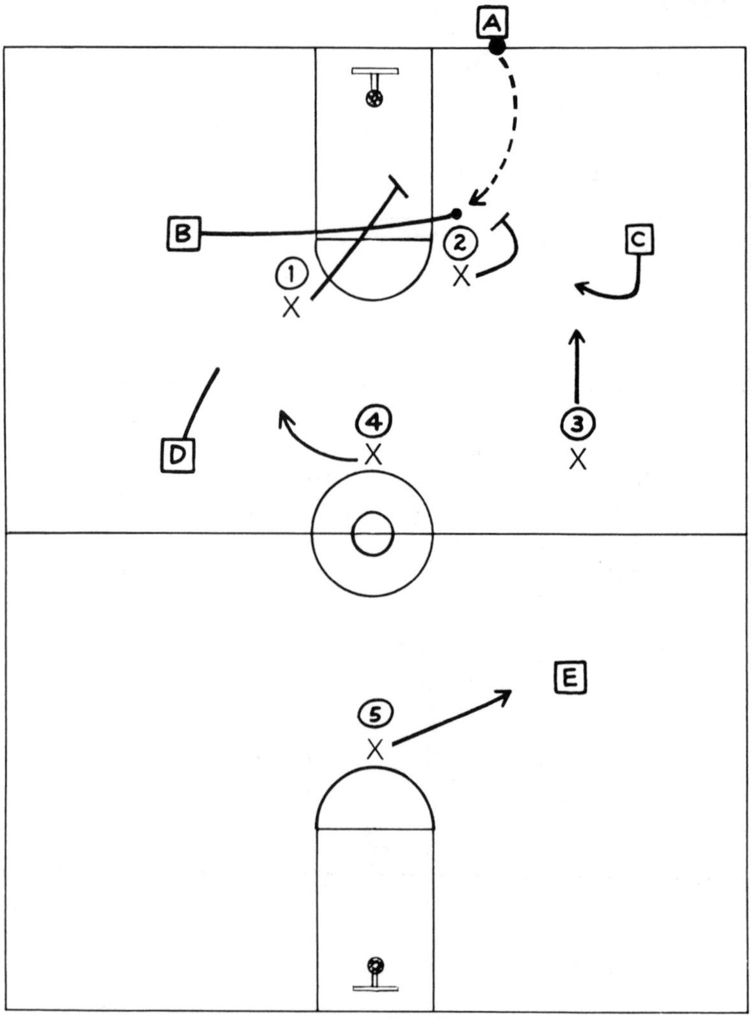

fumble or fall into a trap where a held ball may be called. Although we are interception minded, we try to contain the urge until the opponents make the bad play. Then, we go for the ball and the quick score.

In Chart 136, assuming opponent B made a successful pass to out-of-bounds opponent A who came safely up court, defensive players 1, 2, 3, 4 and 5 will retreat to the Two-One-Two zone as shown above. However, the pressure may again be applied at the ten-second line on a zone press basis.

to a frontcourt or a big man player who may not be as adept in h
the ball as the first receiver.

The initial press is on a man-to-man basis. We will remain
man-to-man or change (on signal) to the zone press as the op]
approach or reach the ten-second line. It is an active defense, a
we often drop back into a passive Two-One-Two zone near the de
basket.

The South Carolina pressure defense is designed to score
It is an organized attempt to force opponents to play our game; t
mistakes—bad passes, hurried and inaccurate passes, travel with t

Chart 136

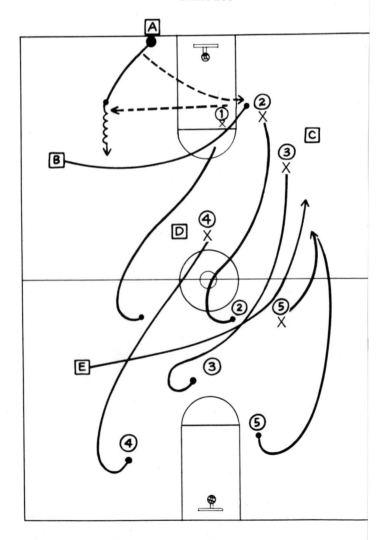

12

game organization, strategy, and scouting

Organization for game day

Coaches who go into a game without a carefully prepared battle plan are begging for trouble. You simply can't leave everything to memory or Providence. To assure an efficient performance by yourself and your team, you must follow a master blueprint—a plan that derives the most from your system and enables you to adjust to any situation or emergency.

The following game-day plan (which will later be broken down into detail) is observed at the University of South Carolina:

GAME DAY PLAN

Locker Room Before Game:

1. Go over offensive scouting notes.

2. Decide on starting lineup.

3. Decide on offense to start in game.

4. Adjustments to be made according to offensive situations.

Style of Game to be Played:

1. *Normal game.*

2. *Control basketball.*

3. *Hold ball back.*

4. *Fast break.*

5. *Semi-press.*

6. *Full-court press.*

Pre-Game Practice:

1. *Warm-up drills.*

2. *Set shooting . . . jump shooting.*

3. *Foul shooting.*

4. *Go to dressing room for final instructions.*

OFFENSIVE GAME STRATEGY

First Time-Out:

1. *Huddle in time-out.*

2. *Players do not talk unless asked a question, or if injured or tired.*

3. *Discuss possible changes in offensive strategy.*

Substitutions:

1. *Reason for substitutions.*

2. *Decision on personal fouls, whether to take out player or to leave him in the game.*

3. *Decision on four personal fouls, whether to take out player or leave him in game until he fouls out.*

Between Halves:

1. *Check score book . . . look over shot chart.*

2. *Tell players of their own personal fouls and of the fouls on the opponents.*

3. Observe leading scorer on other team.

4. Make adjustments in offense if necessary.

5. Give starting lineup for second half.

Decisions:

1. When to freeze ball if we are leading.

2. Plays with seconds to go.

3. Offensive match-ups.

Locker room details

Our team arrives at the dressing room one hour before the game. After the squad has dressed and the trainer has checked each player, we have a meeting.

At this meeting we go over the scouting report for the last time. The names, numbers, heights, and offensive notations are put on a large blackboard so that the players can easily remember the significant details.

We decide on the starting lineup and announce it to the team. This lineup will depend a great deal on the lineup of the opponents. We usually try to start three big men and two smaller men (the regular backcourt men). We may alter this if we intend playing a fast-breaking game.

Our initial offense also depends on the nature of our starting lineup.

Pre-game practice

In warming up before the game we use a three-man passing drill with a lay-up for about five minutes. The purpose of this is to warm up the muscles and to loosen up generally. This part of the practice is supervised by the trainer, who is always present. After this first drill, we take set and jump shots with certain players working on their pivot and hook shots underneath. Finally, the starting team and the first-line substitutes practice their foul shots. Then the squad returns to the dressing room for a final briefing.

OFFENSIVE GAME PROCEDURE

We start the game offense with a modified weave in order to determine the type of defense our opponents are using. Defensively, we start with our basic man-to-man. If the opponents are using a man-to-man defense, we will use our basic Two-Three offense. From this formation we will determine the opponents' reaction to our attack. As they adjust their defense to meet our Two-Three offense, we will shift to a different formation. We will remain in our basic man-to-man defense as long as we can hold our own, preferring to withhold defensive changes until the second half.

Style of game to be played

We mix up the following offenses in a general pattern: single pivot, five-man give-and-go weave, post offense, fast break, and full-court press.

We *play our normal game* whenever our opponents use a basic man-to-man defense, starting off with our regular offense as given above.

We'll *play a control game* whenever our opponents dominate the backboards and are giving us only one shot at the basket. When our opponents are using a running game or are a well-known fast-break team, we try to slow them down by holding on to the ball and taking only good shots. In other words, we try to get the other team to play our style of game. Usually a fast-breaking team isn't familiar with control basketball, and this should work to our advantage.

We'll *hold the ball* against a team superior in manpower and bench strength, and as a change in tactics. This style of game is tremendously disliked by spectators, and can be used only on rare occasions. You will find that the opponents will usually go into a full-court press to try to break it up.

The first time-out

Once the game starts, we let the team play as planned until it becomes necessary to change some of our plans. This we do in the first time-out. Our players huddle in a group in front of our bench, and are taken care of by the trainer. Players do not talk in the huddle unless asked a question or unless one is injured or tired and wants a rest.

During this first and subsequent time-outs, we discuss the strategy to be used; or, if the other team has taken the time-out, we may leave things as they are. Sometimes the work of the scout is thrown out the window at the first time-out. This happens whenever opponents have completely changed the style of play or are using players different from the ones originally scouted.

We try to save our time-outs until the end of the game, when we may need them in order to stop the clock and try some new moves.

Substitutions

The first substitution is usually an important one. With this move, you may change the style of game you have been playing. For example, by substituting a small man for a big man, you might change from a pattern offense to a fast-break attack. Or, by inserting another big man into your lineup, you might switch to a double pivot under the boards. Of course, you do not necessarily have to change your style of play. The first substitute might merely be a replacement for a player who isn't doing too well.

Some coaches will immediately remove a player who picks up three personal fouls; others won't take him out unless it is very close to the end of the half. Experience has proved that foul No. 4 quickly follows foul No. 3, and coaches gamble on this. They may open the second half with the player having three fouls and go along with him until he draws his fourth. At this point, they will yank him out and wait for the closing minutes before putting him in again.

Other coaches believe in leaving a player in regardless of his fouls. They feel that a boy doesn't play as well after a stretch on the bench. This probably will always remain a moot question.

It helps to have a unit in reserve that has been trained in freezing the ball or in throwing up a full-court press. A unit like this will come in handy in the final minutes of a close ball game.

Between halves

During the first half we have one of our managers chart the shots taken by the players of both teams. This shot chart tells us at a glance where the opponents are hitting and enables us to make any needed defensive adjustments.

Together with the score book, the chart tells the story of the first half. From this evidence, plus the intense observation by my assistant and the freshman coaches, who take notes on the bench, we arrive at decisions for the second half. We may stick with the same lineup that finished the first half or we may make certain changes to meet some new situation that has arisen.

We study the score book and tell our players how many personal fouls they have committed and the number on each of our opponents. We warn them about the number of time-outs we took during the first half, and to avoid taking an extra time-out at the expense of a technical foul.

We make certain observations about the leading scorer of the other team and offer suggestions on how to stop him. At this point we may also decide to change our match-ups. If our offense is being stopped, we'll make adjustments—changing our style if necessary. For example, if the other team has a bigger player than our pivot man, we'll stop using a single-pivot offense and put our big man in the corner or at the side, wherever we think he'll work best. This, we hope, will take the opposition's big man away from the defensive boards (if they're playing man-to-man).

Decisions

WHEN TO FREEZE THE BALL WHEN AHEAD. It takes a lot of experience to learn when to go into a freeze and how to operate it. We've been both right and wrong on this matter. It is very difficult to set up any hard and fast rule. It's really a personal matter for the individual coach since he knows the type of player he has and the ability of the team to apply a successful freeze.

We freeze or stall at the end of the game whenever we think our lead is sufficient. We freeze the ball in this manner:

FREEZING THE BALL

1. *We open up the court by keeping the area under the basket open—that is, free from pivot men or post men. We send the big men to the corners or to the baseline.*

2. *We move the ball and the men. We never hold the ball too long, since a man who does so is an easy target for a double-team situation. We sometimes put in another smaller man, an outstanding dribbler, to help freeze the ball.*

3. *We try to eliminate long and cross-court passes.*

4. *We go away from the receiver when passing the ball to prevent double-teaming.*

5. *We stay away from the lane and the ten-second line as much as possible.*

6. *On occasion we use continuity freeze offense with the five men getting into the passing, or a four-man passing freeze with one of the big men setting up a post outside the free-throw lane.*

A common weakness in freezing lies in forgetting to score or not trying to get an easy basket and increase the lead. When the opponents are using a tight man-to-man defense, plays can be worked down the middle and on the sides with a change-up.

SPECIAL PLAYS—WITH SECONDS TO GO. It's advisable to have some plays ready for situations where the clock is running out and your team is down by two or three points. If you don't have the ball, then everything must be done to secure it, such as double-teaming, gambling on interceptions, and possibly fouling the player least likely to convert his free throws. In this case you must get the rebound on the missed try.

The plays with seconds to go should revolve around double and triple screens around the free-throw line. Nearly every coach has these ready for the last seconds. They can be discussed during the time-out near the end of the game. Also, an individual player with drive should be given the ball for the three-point play, his teammates opening up the center of the court under the boards so he can have room to drive.

DEFENSIVE GAME PROCEDURE

It is almost impossible to prepare for the contingencies that may arise in any game, but the coach should prepare and consult a defensive check list to make sure that his team is equipped with counters that will permit his team to meet all possible offensive measures.

At South Carolina University we have found that the offenses used by our competitors differ greatly in application and effectiveness. One team may employ a fine fast break, a driving give-and-go set attack, or a slow, possession offense. Another may use all types of screens and blocks, while still another may feature a big man who is a deadly scorer, or a front line composed of tall, agile players who pound the offensive board.

If we are unable to check these teams by means of our basic man-to-man defense or the screen-switch defense, we will try our Two-One-Two zone, or one of the variations. If none of these can hold the opponents, we may find it necessary to change to some form of the press. We try, of course, to make the opponents play our game or force them to use an offense they cannot apply well.

During the game a bench card may be kept by the assistant coach, a manager, a coaching friend, or an injured player. This card is invaluable in keeping an accurate record of the fouls each player commits and, in general, reflects each player's game performance.

Time outs are valuable. The coach and the players should try to save as many as possible for the final quarter. It is here that the game will be won or lost and where a time out may be invaluable in securing a rest or making a change in strategy.

Just as important in a tough game is the necessity of taking every precaution to enter the final period with the best players on the floor and in good condition. To that end, it is wise to substitute wisely and keep in mind that no game is ever won or lost in the first half. Fatigue increases in direct proportion to the amount of time a player spends in the game. Further, when a player becomes tired, he commits more fouls.

Matching players

Through the years we have given great attention to the matching of players. We feel that our record at St. John's and North Carolina University was helped by careful match-ups. Our coaching staff spends many hours discussing the opposing players in full detail, touching on their strong points and apparent weaknesses. We gather as much information on them as possible and hand it on to the players.

Substitutes sitting on the bench are told to watch the player they might cover later on in the game, and try to pick up something about him. For example, some players can only go to the right. When this is observed by our scout, we suggest to the man assigned to cover him that overshifting to the left may force the opponent to go to *his* left.

Some players are adept at playing a dribbler; therefore, it is wise to match them against good dribblers. Many a game has been won by careful match-ups. While striving for good match-ups defensively, it is also smart to try to force the opponents into bad match-ups. For example, if you have a good tall forward who can play the pivot, you may occasionally pull your center out of the bucket and let the tall forward slip in, particularly if he is being guarded by a small man. An opposing switch may wind up with a small guard on a tall offensive player. An alert offense will quickly exploit the situation by feeding the big man.

Getting the ball

When your team is behind in the closing minutes of a game, it is vital that you get the ball. It is good strategy early in a game against a strong opponent to apply some form of the press to get an idea of the players' ability to meet it. Then when you are going down the stretch the information can be used to good advantage.

We'll use the semi-press against opponents who are poor ball handlers or who take a great deal of time to set up their patterns. We also find this defense effective against single- and double-pivot teams. You must have your players in great physical condition to play a semi-press game.

The full-court press, when used at the start, is considered an offense. We use it as a surprise. We like to spring it against teams that have one or two big men around 6 feet 10 inches. This defense usually forces the opponents to deploy the big men as posts, far away from the offensive basket. This helps destroy their effectiveness, and also puts them into the unaccustomed role of ball handlers. Some coaches take out their big men when the opposition starts with a full-court press.

The time element and the score are of extreme importance in deciding when to go into a full-court press. Once the decision is made, the full-court press should seldom be taken off until the lead is regained. It is easy to commit fouls in a full-court press and you must have the players who can apply the press without excessive fouling. Since the accent is on speed and agility, you'll usually have to take out the big men, except possibly the most agile of them.

The full-court press offers a good change of tactics. It often causes the opponents to lose their poise and make bad and hurried passes. Inasmuch as it is difficult to develop a pattern of play against it, a team caught by surprise will sometimes fall to pieces.

Officials also play an important role in the full-court press. A careful study of them is necessary. Some call them very close, while others are so lenient that they often let the game get away from them. This is, of course, a tremendous advantage to a pressing team.

When the opponents have the ball and are operating a successful freeze a desperate gamble must be made to secure the ball by double-teaming or possibly fouling the player least likely to convert his fouls. In this case, you *must* get the rebound on the missed try.

Coach's defense check list

The preparation of a defensive check list will aid the coach in making sure he has not overlooked certain defensive possibilities; it will also serve to refresh his memory in preparing his team to meet the various game situations. The following check list is presented as a partial guide.

DEFENSIVELY MY PLAYERS ARE PREPARED TO:

1. *Employ and maintain correct defensive positions.*

2. *Play the man without the ball without turning their heads.*

3. *Guard the man with the ball aggressively without fouling.*

4. *Play the cutter, dribbler, and the expert distance marksman.*

5. *Use the half- or the full-man overshift.*

6. *Meet the screen and the block with slides and the switch.*

7. *Force opponents to the sidelines or to the middle.*

8. *Block out effectively in the proper zones.*

9. *Set up the defensive triangle quickly and effectively.*

10. *Rebound efficiently and get the ball into play quickly.*

11. *Collapse to help out with rebounding.*

12. *Apply the sag and the float.*

13. *Close the gate and jam the middle.*

14. *Adjust to match-ups with opponents.*

15. *Work as a team; talk, help out, and WORK.*

16. *Take advantage of double-team opportunities.*

17. *Understand lane play and apply free-throw defense.*

18. *Defend intelligently against out-of-bounds plays.*

19. *Apply the various phases of stopping the fast break.*

20. *Meet jump-ball situations (control the tap or steal the ball).*

21. *Defense the big man (individually and as a team).*

22. *Utilize man-to-man and zone defense variations.*

23. *Use the screen-switch defense.*

24. *Use certain types of the zone defense.*

25. *Employ some forms of combination defenses.*

26. *Apply the man-to-man full-court press and the variations.*

27. *Use the Two-One-Two zone press or a variation.*

28. *Meet the stall and the freeze.*

29. *Utilize the deliberate foul in an ethical manner.*

30. *Defend against the opponents' last-second scoring play.*

Scouting

Scouting information is vital in setting up a defensive plan for a particular opponent. Here, the college coach has a big advantage over the high school mentor. The college coach can employ highly efficient assistants or alumni to scout opponents. With this information as a starter, the college coach can plan months ahead (particularly if the opponent employs the same offensive and defensive styles year after year). The high school coach must rely often upon unqualified scouts and frequently upon little more than hearsay or newspaper accounts. Sometimes he must depend upon the first few minutes of the actual game to gather the required information.

If scouting information is available, the coach should take measures to prepare his team specifically for the various opponents. If information is not available, he must be sure that his team is prepared for the unusual, for the surprise offenses. Scouting information, newspaper results, and team brochures will give the coach some idea of the opponents' scoring potential. If the opponents score consistently in the 80's or 90's, it is foolish to believe that they will not continue to do so. If the coach cannot match a high-scoring team with a high-scoring offense of his own, then, certainly, some effort must be made to hamper the scoring of the opponents.

It is important to know *how* the opponents get their points. Do they concentrate on the fast break? Are the players exceptionally fine marksmen? Do they use the full-court press as an offense? Do they rely upon a high-scoring big man who consistently scores 30 or 40 points? Do the opponents concentrate upon hard-driving tactics to draw fouls and place pressure on the defense? Are set plays the basis for their success? Is the offense built around clever use of screens and blocks? Is the scoring concentrated near the basket? Is the success of the offense based upon fine outside shooters? These are questions for which the coach must find answers. Once the type or types of offense are established, the rest is a matter of preparation and of the efficiency with which the players apply the planned defenses.

If the opponents concentrate on the fast break, it is the responsibility of the coach to be sure that his team is coached in methods of checking the break. Pounding the offensive boards, covering rebounders to stop outlet passes, moving defensive balance players to outlet-pass receiving points, stopping the dribbler, applying the defensive shuttle, getting help, and/or countering with a fast break are important defensive measures.

Should the opponents be great marksmen, it might be wise to use a possession type of game when on the offense and cover the scorers tightly on the defense. In this application, the weak-side guards (on the side of the court away from the ball) might be permitted to float.

In case the opponents employ a full-court press, the coach must equip his team with a counterattack. Countering with a press may help, but it is imperative that the coach prepare his team to meet the press efficiently.

Should the opponents' big man be the menace, some sort of a zone may be called for, or certainly plans should be made to play him in front and on the side when he is near the basket, and in-line when he is in a post position (15 or more feet from the basket).

Should the opponents feature a driving attack down the middle, perhaps a zone, or the screen switch defense, or some type of defense that will jam the middle—such as an overshifting man-to-man defense with sagging and floating—may prove the checking factor.

If the opponents' offense is centered in a set attack with the use of screens and blocks, a zone or the use of floating and sagging and closing the gate may check its effectiveness.

RATING THE OPPONENTS' OFFENSE

1. *Single pivot: describe big man*

2. *Double pivot: describe two big men*

3. *Center open around foul line: designate corner man*

4. *Figure eight: deep; shallow; tight; fast; slow*

5. *Give-and-go style: what two men work the best?*

6. *Fast break: describe outlet passes*

7. *Full-court press offense: describe method*

8. *Rebounding strength: name strong rebounders*

9. *Two-men plays: three-men plays*

10. *Center-tap plays: who gets ball; who scores on tap*

11. *Jump-ball plays*

12. *Out-of-bounds plays*

13. *Delayed attack*

14. *Withholding the ball from play virtually the entire game*

15. *Playing for one shot*

16. *Last-second plays when behind in the score*

17. *Nature of screens: single, double, triple*

18. *Relative speed of team, squad, certain individuals*

19. *Ball handlers, dribblers, quarterbacks*

20. *Zone offenses against various zones; against zone presses*

21. Offenses against certain defenses: collapse, man-to-man, double-teaming the ball, driving the offense into the middle

22. Offense against double-teaming. Reaction to surprise defenses.

In preparing to meet the opponents' defense we must have information concerning the following:

MEETING OPPONENTS' DEFENSE

1. Man-to-man

2. Tight man-to-man

3. Loose man-to-man

4. Switching man-to-man

5. Collapsing man-to-man

6. Tight on the ball; loose away from the ball

7. Zone defense

8. One-Three-One zone

9. Two-One-Two zone

10. Two-Three zone

11. Three-Two zone

12. One-One-Three zone

13. Three-One-One zone

14. Box-and-One

15. Basket hanger with Two-Two

16. Man-to-man with one man playing free

17. Full-court press

18. Semi-court press

19. One-man press

20. Two-man press

21. Zone press

22. Special defenses

23. Double-teaming the ball

24. Forcing the dribbler to sidelines

Scouting individual opponents

The scouting charts with which our scouts are equipped require a report concerning the important skill performances of opposing players. However, there are certain personal qualities which cannot be shown by means of charts. For this reason we like to have thumbnail sketches of each varsity player. These sketches provide insights into personalities: determination, fighting spirit, temper control, impetuousness, calmness under pressure and whether or not the individuals are sleepers, talkers, stargazers, body checkers, head-hunters, and so on.

Personal scouting

When I was at the University of North Carolina it was easy for me to personally scout three of our big rivals—Duke, Wake Forest and North Carolina State. On a night when we were not playing it was merely an hour's drive to one of these schools. However, when it came to opponents who were located at a distance it was a different proposition. A great many coaches do not care to personally scout their opponents. I prefer to get the information first hand; then, I can assume full responsibility for any information or game strategy which may backfire.

Staff scouting

The ideal method is for the entire staff to scout opponents. I like for the assistant coach and the freshman coach to join me in watching our opponents when it is possible for all three of us to be absent from our duties. The duties are divided as follows:

The assistant coach studies and details the opponent's offense, breaking it down into its various formations; he also checks the nature of the fast break.

The freshman coach concentrates on the opponent's defense, paying particular attention to the effectiveness of the defense against the opposing team's type of offense.

The head coach checks the overall strategy of the game with special emphasis on the style of play and the various changes which may be made. He observes the first substitute and the possible reason for the change.

When these three reports are brought together and studied along with the possible acquisition of a past year's movies, a game plan can be prepared. Naturally, much of the scouting material may go out the window should the opponents set up a game plan which is at odds with the notes and preparations you have made. Here, the importance of preparing your team to meet any eventuality is vital.

Scouting services

When it is impossible for the head coach or a member of his staff to scout an opponent it may be advisable to use a scouting service. These services are usually manned by former coaches and/or former players. They do a good job and if contacted in advance can scout the opponent according to your wishes.

Conclusion

Taking all possibilities into account it is my opinion that the personal approach combined with scouting service reports, newspaper reports, movies, and information gleaned from other coaches and players is best. Here, it might be apropos to say that it is wise to have your own team scouted from time to time if possible. It will be interesting, to say the least, to read what others think about your players and your team's style of play.

index

A

Adaptability, team, 8-9
  check list, 9
Administration, school, 1, 2
Advancement, 20-22
Aids, coaching, 9
American Professional League, 3
Arizin, Paul, 36, 37
Assistants, coaching, 5, 14, 17, 197
Athlete's foot, 15
Attack, 8 (*see also* Offense; Zone
  Offenses)
  One-Three-One, 20
  slowing down, 11
  style of, 9
Attacking defensive variations, 108-
  110
Attles, Al, 36, 37

B

Backcourt men:
  in out-of-bounds plays, 96
  in two-man press, 183-184
  in Two-Three offense, 49, 50
Balance, court and defensive, 119

Ball, advancing, 20-22
Basic offense, 19-20, 49, 79
Basketball:
  coach's duty toward, 3
  and the community, 2, 3
  control style, 100-102
  defensive, 3, 11-12
  and educational system, 1
  as game of habits, 5
  inventor of, 180
  offensive, 10-11
  philosophy of, McGuire's, 7-11
  players, 7-8 (*see also* Players)
  professional, 35-37
  rules and, 3
  run-and-fire style, 100-101
  stature of, 111
  system, McGuire, 3
Bee, Clair, 84, 129, 149
Benzoin, Tincture of, 15
Big man:
  against big man, 126-130
  developing skills of, 33-34
  in double-pivot offense, 40-41
  in freeze, 103
  height of, 37
  importance of, on team, 19

as key player in offenses, 33, 51
in offensive defense, 130
in out-of-bounds plays, 96
for pivot-man duties, 51
poise and confidence of, 33-34
press, used against, 185
as rebounder, 165-168
side clear-out and, 60, 61
in single-pivot offense, 38-40 (*see also* Big man offense)
as team defense problem, 126
in Two-Three, 50, 51
use of two in offense (double-pivot), 40-41
utilizing, 33-34
Big-man offense, 33-34, 37-41
Big-man strategy alternatives, 126
Blackboards:
to illustrate situations, 9
at squad meetings, 14
Block dribble, 31
Block plays, against sag and float, 107-108
Bluffing, 93
Boston Celtics, 37
Box-and-One defense, 147-148, 159, 162-164
"Box" offense (*see* One-Two-Two offense)

C

Calisthenics, 15, 17
Camera, use of in coaching, 4
Captains:
and coach, 10, 14
selection of, 13
Chamberlain, Wilt, 36, 37, 38
Change-ups, 31
Circulation, 20, 31-33, 41, 83, 119
Circulation, counter-clockwise, 83
Clinics, coaching, 3
Closing the gate, 125-126
Coaches, 1-7, 9 (*see also* Game day)
assistants (*see* Assistants, coaching)
and big man, 35, 37-38, 40
and captains, 10, 13
as character builders, 7
code for, 1-7
and community, 2
and criticism, 2, 6
and defensive vs. offensive play, 101-102
duty to improve game, 3
enthusiasm for game, 3, 9
as faculty members, 1
and game day, 191
leadership by, 5
newspapers and, 3
and officials, 2, 3
personal characteristics, 2, 3, 6-7
and players, 2, 4, 5, 7-8, 10, 12-13
practice programs and, 5-6
professional, 35-37
public relations and, 2
and quarterbacks, 10
and rules, 2, 4
and school, 2, 3
and scouting, 204
self-belief, 9
and signals, 91-92, 93, 96
and spectators, 2
and sportsmanship, 2, 7
and students, 2
as students of game, 3
and team, 4, 8-9
and time, 5, 9
use of camera, 4
use of movies, 3-4
as youth leaders, 6-7
Coaching, 4, 9-10
assistants (*see* Assistants, coaching)
code of, 1-7
and fundamentals, 4
of individual players, 6
managers (*see* Managers)
planning (*see* Planning)
trainers (*see* Trainers)
Coaching aids, 9
Coaching code, 1-7
Coaching strategies, 111-114

Collapsing man-to-man defense, 131-133
  and "arm's length" principle, 133
  effective use of, 133
  fast break, not used in, 133
  rebounding, 132-133
College basketball, practice, 6
Combination defenses:
  Box-and-One, 147-148, 159, 162-164
  one-man zone, 159, 161-162
  screen-switch, 124, 159-161
  South Carolina University's pressure defense, 188-190
Conditioning, 6, 9, 15, 32 (see also Drills; Practices)
  early-season, 14-15
  in-season, 16
  methods of, 15
  overworking at, 15
Contact, meaning of term, 44
Control game, 100-102
Corner men:
  in out-of-bounds plays, 96
  in Two-Three offense, 49, 50
Court balance, defensive, 122-123
Criticism, 2, 6
Cross, lateral, 64
Cross-country training, 6
Cutting, 31
Cutting lanes, 25-26

D

Deep man, in point zone defense, 152
Defense, 11-12, 111-115 (see also Combination defenses; Man-to-man defense)
  basic principles of, 119-120
  Box-and-One, 147-148, 159, 162-164
  check list, coach's, 199-200
  closing the gate, 125-126
  combination (see Combination defenses)
  consistency in, 113-114
  control game and, 100-102
  fast break, stopping the (see Fast break)
  and high school teams, 114-115
  importance of, 112-113
  jump-ball, 168-172 (see also Jump ball team play)
  lane positions (see Playing the lane)
  man-to-man (see Man-to-man defense)
  one-man zone, 159, 161-162
  opponents' offense, rating, check list, 202-203
  out-of-bonds, 168, 172-176 (see also Out-of-bounds plays)
  plans, 11-12
  Point-and-One, 155-157
  point zone, South Carolina University's (see Point zone defense, South Carolina University)
  press (see Press)
  procedure for defensive game, 197-205
  retreating, 123, 124
  sag and float, 125, 126, 149
  screen-switch, 124, 159-161
  and signals, 91-92
  South Carolina University's point zone (see Point zone defense, South Carolina University's)
  surprise moves, 21-22, 179, 180, 181, 183, 198-199
  Two-One-Two zone press (see Press)
  of under-basket area, 126-130
  unexplored possibilities in, 114
  variations in, 108-110, 124-126
  versus offense, 101-102 (see also Defensive philosophy)
  zone (see Zone defense)
Defense check list, coach's 199-200
Defensing the big man, 126-130 (see also Big-man strategy alternatives)
  collapsing defense, 129

double-teaming, 128-129
full-court press, 129
playing between ball and man,
128
playing pivot man three-quarters, 128
zone defense, 129
Defensive areas (zones), 120-122
Defensive break, 116
Defensive code, 115-117
Defensive game procedure, 197-205
Defensive philosophy, a, 111-115
Defensive team principles, 119-124
Defensive variations, attacking,
108-110 (*see also* Offense)
Diet, 17-18
meals, players', *suggested menus*,
18
Discipline, 5-6, 8, 17
Double-pivot offense (*see* Big-man
offense)
Dribble-block, 31
Dribbling:
against the press, 105
block, 31
to block sag and float, 107-108
in fast break, 23, 25, 28, 29
in fast breaking attack, 135-138
in five-man roll, 43
in four-man roll with post-pivot,
44, 45, 47
in freeze, 102-103
in weave plays, 42
Drills (*see also* Conditioning; Practices)
to develop fundamentals, 5, 15
early-season, 15
fast-break, 15
freedom "breaks," 15
freeze, 103
full-press, 15
fun, 5
fundamental, 5, 20
medicine-ball, 15
passing, 15
possession, 102
repetition of, 5

three-man passing, 6
time schedule for, 15
Drinking rule, 17

E

Eastern style offense, 19, 24
Eating, 17 (*see also* Diet; Meals)
Equipment, inspection of, 13
Exercising, 6 (*see also* Calisthenics)

F

Faculty, and coach, 1, 2
Fast break, 22-31
and collapsing defense, 132
in defense, 134, 165
dribbling in, value of, 23, 135
from man-to-man defense, 22
from unsuccessful free throw, 29
in offense, 10, 22, 133
passing in, 23
principles of 23-25
stopping tactics, 133-138; South
Carolina University's, 134-138
tips, 30-31
types, 133
and zone defense, 22
Feet, care of, 6, 15
Five-man give-and-go weave, 41-
42, 109
Five-man roll, 43-44
Float, 107-108, 125, 126, 149
Fouls, 44, 195, 197
Four-man roll with post-pivot, 44-
47
Fox, Jim, 38
Free-throw line, width of, 126
Freeze, meeting the, 176-177
Freezing, 11, 102-104, 196
in five-man roll, 43
in give-and-go weave, 31
methods, 102-103
tips, 104
Full-court press (*see* Press)

Fundamentals, 10, 20
  drills in, 5, 20
  importance of, 4, 5
Fun drills, 5

G

Game day:
  between halves, 195-196
  decisions, 196
  defense *check list*, coach's 199-200
  defensive game procedure, 197-205
  first time-out, 194
  freezing the ball, 196
  getting the ball, 198
  locker room details, 193
  matching players, 198
  meeting opponents' defense, *check list*, 203-204
  offensive game procedure, 193-197
  offensive game strategy, 192-193
  organization for, 191-193
  plan, 191-193
  pre-game practice, 193
  rating opponents' offense, *check list*, 202-203
  scouting, 200-205
  special plays—with seconds to go, 197
  style of game to be played, 194
Games:
  coach's responsibility, 3, 12
  officiating at, 3
  rules and, 3
Game signals, 91-92
Give-and-go weave, 21-33
Gola, Tom, 36, 37
Gymnasium, inspection of, 13

H

Health, of players, 1-2, 10
Height (of big man), 37

Held-ball plays, 95 (*see also* Jump-ball team play)
Helping man-to-man defense (*see* Support man-to-man defense)
High school teams and defense, 114-115, 116

I

Injuries:
  coach's responsibility, 2, 5
  treatment of, 2
  In-line principles (*see* Man-to-man defense)
Inside rebound area, 25
Inside screen, 31, 43, 107-108 (*see also* Screens)
Interception, 43
Isometric exercises, 6

J

Jayvee squad, 8
Jump-ball team play, 91-95, 168-172 (*see also* Defense; Tap)
  center-jump play, 95
  defense plays, 168-172
  development of plays from, 92-93
  formation for, 93, 172
  front-court play, 93-94
  possession of ball, 92, 93
  and signals, 91-92

L

Lane, playing the, 100, 165-168
Lanes:
  cutting, 25-26
  zone-press, 186-187
Lateral cross, 64
Leadership, coaching, 5
Leg power, 6, 13, 15
Locker room, supervision of, 5
Long-pass area, 25

M

McGuire, Frank, 3, 37
  basketball philosophy, 7-11
  on defense system, 3, 11-12
Managers, 5, 14, 195, 197
  duties of, 13
  selection of, 13
  and weight chart, 17
Man-to-man defense (*see also* Com-
    bination defenses; Defense)
  advantages of, 138-139
  as basic defense, 115-117
  collapsing (*see* Collapsing man-
    to-man defense)
  disadvantages of, 145-146
  in-line principles, 120, 133
  loose, 131
  offensive, 130
  and players, 117
  press (*see* Press)
  rebounding, 132-133, 139
  at South Carolina University,
    115-116, 147
  support (*see* Support man-to-
    man defense)
  variations of, 12, 130-133
Meals, players', *sample menus*, 18
Medicine ball, 15, 33
Meetings:
  check list for, 14
  squad, 14, 16
  staff, 14
Menus, suggested (players'), 18
Movement, player, 31
Movies:
  of games, 3, 4
  of players, 4

N

Naismith, Dr. James A., inventor of
    basketball, *quoted,* 180
National Basketball Association
    (NBA), 35, 36
Newspapers, 2
Night practices, 10

North Carolina, University of, 3, 38,
    204

O

Offense, 10-11
  against defensive variations, 108-
    110
  against One-Three-One zone, 84-
    86
  against One-Two-Two zone, 87-
    88
  against point zone defense, 152-
    155
  against press, 104-107
  against sag and float, 107-108
  against switching defense, 108-
    110
  against Three-Two zone, 89
  against Two-One-Two zone:
    using 1-3-1, 83-84
    using 2-1-2, 89-90
  against Two-Three zone, 81-82
  basic, 19-20, 49, 79 (*see also*
    Two-Three offense)
  big-man, 33-34, 37-41
  changing to another offense, 91
  check list, 11
  control game and, 100-102
  double-pivot, 40-41
  Eastern style, 19
  fast break in, 10, 22-31, 79
  five-man give-and-go weave, 41-
    42, 109
  five-man roll, 43-44
  four-man roll with post-pivot, 44-
    47
  give-and-go weave, 31-33
  man-to-man, 19-20
  One-Three-One, 20, 79-80, 81-86
  One-Two-Two, 62-78
  opponents' defense, meeting,
    check list, 203-204
  pressure, 9
  procedure for offensive game,
    193-197
  roll (*see* Rolls)

and signals, 91-92
single-pivot, 38-40
South Carolina University's (*see*
Big-man offense)
strategy (*see* Game day)
Three-Two, 19
Two-Three, 19-20, 35, 38-40, 49-
62, 109 (*see also* Two-Three
offense)
Two-Two-One, 79-80
versus defense style, 101-102 (*see*
also Control game; Defensive
philosophy)
zone, 79-90 (*see also* Zone offenses)
Offensive game procedure, 193-197
Offensive game strategy, *outline*,
192-193
Officials, 2, 3, 199
One-man zone defense, 159, 161-
162
One-on-one play:
value of, in Two-Three offense,
49-50
One-Three-One zone offense, 20,
79-80 81-86
One-Two-Two offense, 62-78
Opponents' defense, meeting, *check*
list, 203-204
Opponents' offense, rating, *check*
list, 202-203
Out-of-bounds plays, 95-100, 168,
172-176
assignment of players, 96
formations for, 96
importance of, 95-96
options in, 96
sideline, 96
Outside screen, 31, 33, 43 (*see also*
Screens)
Overcoaching, 9

P

Parents:
coach's relationship with, 2
permission of, 14

and players' diet, 17-18
Passes:
in fast break, 23
in freeze, 103
and give-and-go weave, 31
in out-of-bounds plays, 96
short, 80
timing of, teaching, 31
Philadelphia Warriors, 3, 35, 36, 37,
38
Philosophy of basketball, a, 7-11
Physicians, 2, 10, 17
Pivot man, 20, 49, 126 (*see also*
Positions)
big man as, 51 (*see also* Big-man
offense)
in give-and-go weave, 34-35
as key man in Two-Three offense, 51
in point zone defense, 152
and practice, 34
in Two-Three offense, 49
Planning:
in-season, 5
of practice sessions, 5, 7-8
pre-season, 12-13
the season, 12-17
Players, 7-8 (*see also* Game day)
backcourt (*see* Backcourt men)
big (*see* Big man)
camera shots of plays by, 3-4
conditioning of, 9 (*see also* Conditioning)
and control game, 101-102
corner (*see* Corner men)
criticism of, 6
and defensive play, 102, 115
diet (*see* Diet)
discipline of, 5-6, 8
duties of, 4
enthusiasm of, 7-8, 13
exercising (*see* Exercising)
fun drills for, 5
health of, 1-2, 10
and horseplay, 5
individual, coaching of, 6
injuries of, 2, 91

jayvee, 8
and man-to-man defense, 115-117
matching, 198
and offensive play, 102
overplaying of, 8
parents of, 2, 4
personal character of, 7
pivot, or post (see Pivot man)
and practices (see Practices)
pre-season activities, 6, 12-13
relations with coach, 4, 6-7
reserve, 8
and signals, 91-92, 93, 96
and sportsmanship, 2
tall (see Big man)
and tap (see Taps)
and team spirit, 4, 5, 8
time-outs, 91, 194, 197
training of, 1-2, 10, 16-18
Playing the lane, 100, 165-168
Point-and-One defense, 155-157
Point man, in point zone defense, 151
Point zone defense, South Carolina University's, 149-155
basic principles of, 149
formations, 149
meeting attacks against, 152-155
objectives of, 151
player responsibilities in, 151-152
positions, 151-155
unique features, 149
Positions:
in big-man offense, 38-41
in control game, 101-102
in double-pivot offense, 40-41
in freeze, 102-103
in give-and-go weave, 31
jump-ball, 93, 172
in One-Two-Two offense, 62
in One-Three-One zone offense, 81
in out-of-bounds plays, 96
in point zone defense, 151-155
in single-pivot offense, 38-40
in Two-Three offense, 51

Possession, 198, 199
Possession tap, 92, 93 (see also Tap)
Post man (see Pivot man)
Post-pivot man (see Pivot man)
Post screens, 50 (see also Screens)
Practice programs, 5-6, 16
Practices, 10 (see also Conditioning; Drills)
after first home game, 16
early-season, 14-15
following meals, 17
fun in, 5, 7
in-season program, 16
night, 10
outline for, 14
overworking, 15, 16
planning of (see Planning)
pre-game, 193
pre-season, 6
program for, 16
restricted period (college), 6
Pre-game procedures (see Game Day)
Pre-season activities, 6, 12-13, 14
Press, 104-107, 179-180
against big men, 184
attacking, 105-107
comment on, by inventor of basketball, 180
defense positioning in, 182
dribbler as key to, 105
full-court, 179, 180, 181-182, 198-199
full-court, as starting surprise, 198-199
lanes, zone-press, 186-187
preparing for, 105-106
semi-, 186, 198
single-man, 179-180, 183
South Carolina University's combination, 188-190
three-quarter, 184-185
two-man, 183-184
Two-One-Two zone, 186
types of, 104
variations of, 183-190

when to use, 181-182, 184
zone, 186
Pressure offense (*see* Offense)
Professional basketball, 35-37
Publicity, 2
Public relations, 2

Q

Quarterbacks:
backcourt players regarded as, 50
and coach, 10
in zone offense, 80

R

Rebound areas, 25-26
Rebounding, 132-133, 139, 165-168
Repetition, importance of, 5
Reserve players, 8
Restricted practice (college), 6
Retreating defense, 122
Retreating methods, 119, 124
Roadwork, 17
Rodgers, Guy, 36
Rolls:
against switching defense, 109
five-man, 43-44
four-man with post-pivot, 44-47
Rope-skipping, 6, 15, 33
Rosenbluth, Lenny, 38
Rules:
coach's obligations, 3
training (*see* Training rules)
Run-and-fire versus control game, 100-101

S

Safety area for rebounders, 25
Sag, 107-108, 125, 126, 149
St. John's University, 3, 38, 40
Scouting:
by the coach, 204
by the staff, 204
of individual opponents, 204

to learn opponents' zone defenses, 79
of opponents, 7, 121-122, 200-205
services, 205
Screen-switch defense, 124, 159-161
Screens:
inside, 31, 43, 107-108
outside, 31, 33, 43
post, 50
Semi-press (*see* Press)
Shadow boxing, 15
Short-pass area, 25
Side clear-out, 60-61
Signals, game, 91-92, 93, 96
Single-man press (*see* Press)
Single-pivot offense (*see* Big-man offense)
Skills, basic, 10
Skull sessions, 9
Sleep, 17
Smoking rule, 17
South Carolina, University of, 3, 10, 20, 31, 33, 37, 38, 41, 79, 93, 102, 105, 113, 131, 134, 145, 147, 159, 162, 179, 189, 191
South Carolina University's fast break defense (*see* Fast break)
South Carolina University's offense (*see* Big-man offense)
South Carolina University point zone defense (*see* Point zone defense)
South Carolina University's pressure defense, 188-190 (*see also* Press)
Special plays—with seconds to go, 197
Sportsmanship:
in coaching, 2, 7
in players, 2
Squad meetings, 14, 16
Stadiums, 37
Staff meetings, *check list*, 14
Stall, meeting the, 177-178
Strategies, coaching, 111-114
Strategy board, 9
Style, game, 194

Substitutions, 195
Support man-to-man defense,
139-145
  advantage of, over zone, 139
  other terms for, 139
  rebounding, defensive, 139
Surprise moves, 21-22, 179, 180, 181,
183, 198-199
Switching defense, attacking the,
108-110
System, McGuire, 3

T

Tall man (*see* Big man; Height)
Tap:
  back, 95
  center, 92, 93
  controlled by opponents,
168-169
  deep back, 93, 95
  when lost, 172
Team:
  adaptability, 8, 9
  coach and, 4
  and control game, 101
  spirit of, 5
Three-man passing drill, 6 (*see also*
Drill)
Three-quarter press, 184-185 (*see
also* Press)
Three-Two offense, 19
Time, importance of, 59
Time-outs, 91, 194, 197
Tincture of Benzoin, 15
Trainers, 5, 10, 14, 16, 17
Training:
  cross-country, 6
  diet requirements, 17-18
  drinking, 17
  health and, 1-2, 10
  rules (*see* Training rules)
  smoking, 17
Training rules, 10, 16-18
  importance of, 4
  violation of, 17
Two-man press (*see* Press)

Two-One-Two zone press (*see*
Press)
Two-Three offense,, 19-20, 35, 38-
40, 49-62
  against switching defense, 109
  big man as key player, 51
  pivot man in, 51
  position responsibilities, 49
  positions in, 51
Two-Two-One zone offense, 79-80,
86-88

U

Under-basket defense strategy,
126-130

V

Visitation Triangles, 3
Volleyball, 17

W

Weaves, 31-33, 41-42
Weight chart, keeping of, 17
Weight problems, 17
Wing men, in point zone defense,
151
Wing variation, in One-Two-Two
offense, 73
Workouts, 5, 15 (*see also* Drills;
Practices)

Z

Zone defense, 79, 147-158 (*see also*
Combination defense;
Defense
  advantages of, 157-158, 168
  bunched (opponents')
  for center jump, 170-171
  disadvantages of, 158
  at South Carolina University,
116-117
  versus support man-to-man, 139

Zone formations, opponents', 80
Zone offenses, 79-90
    basic, 79-80
    One-Three-One, 79-80, 81-86
    opponents' zone formations, 80

Two-Two-One, 79-80, 86-88
Zone press (*see* Press)
Zone-press lanes, 186-187 (*see also*
    Lanes; Press)
Zones, defensive, 120-122

DATE DUE